The Burning Cauldron of Fiery Fire

Anne Washburn

methuen | drama
LONDON • NEW YORK • OXFORD • NEW DELHI • SYDNEY

METHUEN DRAMA

Bloomsbury Publishing Plc, 50 Bedford Square, London, WC1B 3DP, UK
Bloomsbury Publishing Inc, 1359 Broadway, New York, NY 10018, USA
Bloomsbury Publishing Ireland, 29 Earlsfort Terrace, Dublin 2,
D02 AY28, Ireland

BLOOMSBURY, METHUEN DRAMA and the Methuen
Drama logo are trademarks of Bloomsbury Publishing Plc.

First published in Great Britain 2025

Copyright © Anne Washburn, 2025

Anne Washburn has asserted her right under the Copyright, Designs
and Patents Act, 1988, to be identified as Author of this work.

Cover designed by June Buck, Vineyard Theatre

Cover image created with felt and photographed by June Buck

All rights reserved. No part of this publication may be: i) reproduced or transmitted in any form, electronic or mechanical, including photocopying, recording or by means of any information storage or retrieval system without prior permission in writing from the publishers; or ii) used or reproduced in any way for the training, development or operation of artificial intelligence (AI) technologies, including generative AI technologies. The rights holders expressly reserve this publication from the text and data mining exception as per Article 4(3) of the Digital Single Market Directive (EU) 2019/790.

Bloomsbury Publishing Plc does not have any control over, or responsibility for, any third-party websites referred to or in this book. All internet addresses given in this book were correct at the time of going to press. The author and publisher regret any inconvenience caused if addresses have changed or sites have ceased to exist, but can accept no responsibility for any such changes.

No rights in incidental music or songs contained in the work are hereby granted and performance rights for any performance/presentation whatsoever must be obtained from the respective copyright owners.

All rights whatsoever in this play are strictly reserved and application for performance etc. should be made before rehearsals to United Talent Agency, 888 Seventh Avenue, FL. 7, New York, NY 10106; +1 (212) 659–2600.
No performance may be given unless a licence has been obtained.

A catalogue record for this book is available from the British Library.

A catalog record for this book is available from the Library of Congress.

ISBN: PB: 978-1-3506-2519-8
ePDF: 978-1-3506-1386-7
eBook: 978-1-3506-1387-4

Series: Modern Plays

Typeset by Mark Heslington Ltd, Scarborough, North Yorkshire

For product safety related questions contact
productsafety@bloomsbury.com.

To find out more about our authors and books visit
www.bloomsbury.com and sign up for our newsletters.

The Burning Cauldron of Fiery Fire had its world premiere at The Vineyard Theatre (Sarah Stern, Artistic Director) in a co-production with The Civilians (Steve Cosson, Artistic Director) on 23 October 2025. It had the following cast and creative team:

Jeff Biehl, Simon
Bartley Booz, Paul
Cricket Brown, Gracie
Donnetta Lavinia Grays, Diana
Bruce McKenzie, Thomas
Bobby Moreno, Milo
Tom Pecinka, Will
Marianne Rendón, Mari

Anne Washburn, Writer
Steve Cosson, Director
Andrew Boyce, Scenic Design
Emily Rebholz, Costume Design
Amith Chandrashaker, Lighting Design
Ryan Gamblin, Sound Design & Composition
Tommy Kurzman, Wig & Hair Design
Monkey Boys Productions, Puppet Design
Steve Cuiffo, Special Effects Consultant
Nehemiah Luckett, Songs & Vocal Arrangements
Dan Sander-Wells, Music Direction
Henry Russell Bergstein, CSA and Serafina Tiranno-Cimisi, CSA, Casting Directors
Esti Bernstein, Production Stage Manager

The world premiere production of *The Burning Cauldron of Fiery Fire* was produced by Vineyard Theatre (Sarah Stern, Artistic Director, Moogie Brooks, Managing Producer) and The Civilians (Steve Cosson, Artistic Director, Margaret Moll, Managing Director), New York City, 2025.

The Burning Cauldron of Fiery Fire was developed at the Ojai Playwrights Conference: Jeremy B. Cohen, Producing Artistic Director.

We would like to thank Actors Theater of Seattle (ACT), especially John Langs, and the 2022 resident company, for a productive workshop on intentional communities and early material from the play.

The Burning Cauldron of Fiery Fire

The play is cast with 8 adult actors.

Those 8 adult actors will play 18 adults, and 8 children.

(Some of those adult actors will play children acting the role of adults.)

The adults look, well, kind of like hippies: the men with long hair and beards, the women a little long haired and drapey. Will looks unplaceable, not like a hippie, but not-not like a hippie.

A Ghazal is a very old Persian poetic form. An example of which is seen in the text.

Sonic elements are in bold.

Not a moment of this should be played for satire. Give everyone full credit.

The Many Roles in the order of their speaking:

MILO, *6. Also:* **ADULT MILO**, *mid 30s. Also:* **SHORT WIZARD**, *and* **CHORAL** – (5).

MARI, *20s or 30s. Also:* **LAUREL**, *8. Also:* **PAGE** *and* **CHORAL** – (1).

PETER, *20s or 30s. Also* **WILL**, *a few years older. Also:* **ROBERT**, *5 and* **CHORAL** – (8).

THOMAS, *50s or 60s. Also:* **MARA**, *3 and* **CHORAL** – (7).

DIANA, *40s. Also:* **CRYSTAL**, *9. Also:* **KING** *and* **CHORAL** – (3).

GRACIE, *20s. Also:* **TANYA**, *9. Also:* **PRINCESS** *and* **CHORAL** – (6).

SIMON, *40s. Also:* **ROLF**, *7,* **PAGEANT NARRATOR**, **HEN**, *and* **CHORAL** – (2).

GHAZAL, *20s. Also:* **PAUL**, *20s. Also:* **ADAM**, *7,* **PAGEANT PETER**, *and* **CHORAL** – (4).

Sometimes there are Choral Voices. They will generally speak singularly, rather than in union, although that should happen too sometimes.

CHORAL – 1 Is that smoke?

CHORAL – 3, 4 Or fog

CHORAL – 2 Fog

CHORAL – 3, 4, 6 Fog and woodsmoke

CHORAL – 6 A deer

CHORAL – 3 Another deer

The play begins in a swirl of incident: a woman, a man, a child.

MILO Auuugh

Pointing, accusing:

Peter is scaring me!

MARI What?

MILO Peter is scaring me!

PETER Milo wrecked my painting. He did it deliberately.

MILO I was helping!

CHORAL – 3 Artichokes, pumpkins

CHORAL – 4 Thistles

CHORAL – 2 Great Horned Owl

MARI You didn't hit him

PETER I didn't no

MARI Did he – (*Shushing* **PETER**.) shhhhhhhh – what happened. What happened Milo?

PETER Yes tell her what happened.

MARI Shhhhh.

CHORAL – 6   Gopher holes

CHORAL – 7   Goat turds

CHORAL – 3, 6   Live Oak

CHORAL – 3   Eucalyptus

MARI   What –

Wiping **MILO**'s *face, soothing gestures –*

MARI   what happened?

MILO   I saw plums. So I put plums into it. I saw – in my (*Taps forehead.*) I saw it would be better. So I added them I mixed colors first.

PETER   The entire palette *smeared* – do you know how long it takes to mix a palette it's an act of art *unto itself*.

Fierce silencing gesture from **MARI**.

MARI   Did you paint, onto his painting.

MILO   Uh huh. I was *helping*.

MARI   You were helping. That was a beautiful – it's *wonderful* when we help . . .

MILO   Uh huh.

PETER *has kind of sunk into a despair.*

CHORAL – 7   Hill sage

CHORAL – 4   Crows

CHORAL – 3   Red Tailed Hawk

CHORAL – 6   Bay

MARI   And it's wonderful that you saw plums, in your mind, and you put those plums . . . into the world.

MILO (*agreement*)   Uh huh.

PETER *looks incredulous.*

She's trying to figure out how to get to the next bit.

PETER   He knew what he was doing, it wasn't inspiration that was *vandalism*.

MILO   I was helping! The plums are so beautiful! Your painting is dumb! That painting is so dumb!

PETER *rears up in outrage, frustration.*

PETER   Gaaaaaaaagh!

MILO *cries out in mute rage/fear she clutches him to her.*

MARI   Go! Go! Your anger is just – (*Can't express it or even figure it out.*) – go! Go away!

MILO *worked up by all of this into hysterics shrieking senselessly almost to himself:*

MILO   *Go Away!*

CHORAL – 3, 6   Redwood

CHORAL – 2   Hemlock

CHORAL – 6   Creek

CHORAL – 3   Sunflowers

CHORAL – 4, 7   Asters

CHORAL – 2, 6   Yarrow

CHORAL – 3   Squash

CHORAL – 2   How many species of

CHORAL – 2, 3, 4, 6, 7   coastal pine?

ADULT MILO   I did it deliberately it was absolutely an act of mischief

As well as art criticism: it did need purples

CHORAL – 7   Old tractor

CHORAL – 6   New tractor

CHORAL – 4 Middle-aged tractor.

CHORAL – 2, 3, 4 An old headlight in the grass

CHORAL – 2 Who left The Gate unlatched??

CHORAL – 4 Not me!

ADULT MILO *I* needed purples. I could see the plums in my mind's eye perfect spheres of perfect gleaming – painting plums was wanting to taste plums but more wanting to take that rich dark shifting coloration inside myself to incorporate plums into my very being – I craved something . . . sweet . . . and kind of extraordinary . . .

CHORAL – 4 The hoe left in the chard row: dew

CHORAL – 3 rust

CHORAL – 3, 4 more dew, plums

ADULT MILO and I was only allowed to use kid paints tempura paints so easy to wash out and away so crude in their expression so limited in the range of color they could attain I was forbidden those alluring oil paints the rich saturated hues the heaviness the thick squidge squozen from the wonderful soft metal tubes.

And it was a dumb painting it needed purple plums and I was supposed to be helpful and creative and think outside the box and also, I don't know, I didn't like Peter didn't like his droopiness I found him irritating he hadn't once played with me or roughhoused and anyway I knew I could get away with it.

If I acted like an angel an artist

I knew there was very little I couldn't get away with.

CHORAL – 7 Boughs thick with plums.

CHORAL – 3 Plums on the grass, in the road.

CHORAL – 4 Doe.

CHORAL – 2, 5 Faun

CHORAL – 7 And then another faun

CHORAL – 1, 3 We should make jam from these right we should make liquor like they do in the Balkans when will we find a way to attend to all these

CHORAL – 3 wonderful

CHORAL – 2, 4, 5 wild plums

CHORAL – 3 before they

CHORAL – 5 fall

CHORAL – 7 and rot

CHORAL – 2 a wildcat skull:

CHORAL – 4 roses in the sockets

CHORAL – 1 (oh the children did that)

CHORAL – 3 Deer scatter up the hillside

CHORAL – 2 Red Shouldered Hawk, circling

CHORAL – 5, 6 Fog, and smoke

CHORAL – 2, 6 And smoke in the fog

CHORAL – 1, 5, 6 and fog in the smoke

Sound of a crackling fire.

Which cuts out very abruptly, and very completely.

Night, mist, **THOMAS** *kneels, holding a carboard box of matches. The rest of the community is gathered behind him, standing, illuminating the earth ahead of him with flashlights we can't really see their faces.*

THOMAS We have been, favored, in our time together, with three births – each one glorious. A birth increases us, and joins us together in celebration.

10   The Burning Cauldron of Fiery Fire

This is our first death. We are subtracted, in an important and cruel way.

We are the stronger for it.

A collective takes joy in one another. A community sorrows together. A *community* gathers its dead and commends them to God.

I'm not going to 'talk about the man we knew'.

Because we all knew him.

Because it's impossible to know anyone and I won't try to round into a smooth and coherent story a wild and diverse phenomenon. Smoke. Fog. I knew Peter like a brother but I'm sure it's as truthful to say that I hardly knew him as it is to say that I know all of you so well, and barely.

Yesterday, Peter was alive. He walked among us with a beating heart. If you'd asked me what do you love about Peter I would have said: his heart.

But I don't think I ever looked at him and thought: Peter . . . your heart is *beating.*

Man I wish I had.

I'm what I'm trying to say I didn't cherish

the earth in him all these years of millions of years of biology star fragments remorseless series of cell divisions and . . . fucking . . . perishing . . . which led to him.

We know his soul lives on but he will never again be this creature.

Listen. Listen. What is that sound. Listen. Carefully. Listen:

the beating

the all but silent booming

of twenty-six

bleeding

The Burning Cauldron of Fiery Fire 11

grieving

hearts.

And then he lights a match.

Lights flare and flare and raise and

Then drop to a dim.

Dawn.

CHORAL – 3 Great Horned Owl

CHORAL – 6 Another Great Horned Owl

CHORAL – 4 Crow

CHORAL – 3 Concerned conversation between two Great Horned Owls

CHORAL – 5 The tingling start of Dawn

CHORAL – 6 The one Great Horned Owl flies away in one direction

CHORAL – 3 The other Great Horned Owl flies away in another direction

CHORAL – 6 Spotted Towhee

CHORAL – 2 Then American Robin

CHORAL – 4 Crow

CHORAL – 1, 2 Now Steller's Jay

CHORAL – 2, 6 Song Sparrow joins in

CHORAL – 6, 7 Scrub Jay joins in

CHORAL – 5 First light. The Dawn Chorous.

CHORAL – 3, 4, 5 Next: Northern House Wren

CHORAL – 7, 1, 2 Now Dark-eyed Junco

CHORAL – 2, 3, 4 Wrentit piles on

CHORAL – 3, 4, 5   California Towhee

CHORAL – ALL (but 8)   Northern Flicker

Townsend Warbler

Raven

CHORAL – 4   Crow

CHORAL – ALL (but 8)   Chestnut backed chickadee

CHORAL – 4   Crow

CHORAL – ALL (but 8)   Red shouldered Hawk

Hairy Woodpecker

CHORAL – 5   Light. Fog. A gray morning.

CHORAL – 4   Crows

A conclave of crows heard first above and all around us, and then, muted heard from inside.

CHORAL – 2   The green couch, the firm couch, the saggy couch

CHORAL – 6, 3, 2   Muddy boots on the porch

CHORAL – 1, 5, 4   Coffee cups in the sink.

CHORAL – 6, 7, 3   The ponging of the woodstove.

CHORAL – 6   On the underside of the firm couch a small cluster of spider infants.

CHORAL – 4   Crows. The crows think they have found something interesting. Down there on the ground.

THOMAS   Paul has most kindly volunteered to . . . keep watch over Peter while we deliberate.

DIANA   A cup of coffee?

THOMAS   I've had a lot of coffee. (*An internal calculation.*) I could have more coffee.

DIANA *returns after a moment with a blue ceramic mug of coffee.*

DIANA   Does Paul need more coffee?

THOMAS   I offered, he said no.

THOMAS *sits. After a moment he sips. He sips.*

DIANA (*making an effort to speak pragmatically*)   I think the first question is: do we re-burn him, or do we bury him as is.

THOMAS   That was his pyre. It wasn't to obliterate him. It was to honor him.

GRACIE   So we bury him?

SIMON   He's too clumpy to scatter.

GRACIE *utters a small kind of cry.*

SIMON   Crematoriums are . . . it's very specialized . . .

DIANA   So we're not going to try again.

THOMAS   That would be a mockery. No one reburns their dead.

SIMON   And we're unlikely to get much further unless we really pile on the fuel which after last night I don't much fancy I'm going to put it out there that the next time we, burn, one of our own, or anything else for that matter, we've got to have buckets of water, buckets of dirt, lots of them, we've got to have a protocol for all outdoor fires sacred or profane that was a bad moment when the blaze spread, if the wind had come up? Those hills are tinder.

MARI   Alright, Simon.

SIMON   We'll bury him now but . . . very deeply and very carefully. There's meat on him still and he will attract . . . the appetite of many.

Pause while they all digest that.

THOMAS I wonder if there's something in that. In yielding to the appetite of Nature. I think that might have interested Peter, might have really appealed to him.

Gives it a beat.

SIMON Nature won't be tidy.

DIANA No.

SIMON Bones will be quarreled over and dragged away, washed downstream and onto the beach. When a dog trots up to someone with a femur the cops get interested.

DIANA So it *was* a crime

SIMON It was probably a crime. Technically. It was definitely extralegal.

GRACIE But a marker. Do we not have a marker?

THOMAS The entire earth is his marker. We're not going to have a marker.

GRACIE We need to know where he *is* though. Even if it's not marked.

DIANA So just to be clear: we're acknowledging, right, that what we have done was right – was definitely right – but

THOMAS But the world wants us to have called the authorities, the authorities want to take Peter away and stash him on an ice tray in a morgue.

SIMON To give to the family.

THOMAS And they're not having him. He would never want them to have him.

DIANA And I agree I'm not saying we did the wrong thing, I'm saying we did the thing which is less simple.

SIMON It has become . . . complex to explain.

THOMAS The decision which we made collectively – and we did make it collectively – was made in great emotion and, like a lot of decisions made in great emotion, it was very satisfactory, but um . . .

then there's a lot of responsibility around it.

There is a moment or two.

GRACIE   What about his things. If we burned his bones, or if we tried to burn his bones do we burn his things?

Bit of a pause.

SIMON   Right. Good question.

DIANA (*trying it out*)   Burn them . . .

GRACIE (*also trying to think it through*)   Would he have wanted us to burn them.

SIMON   He in many ways lost the right to have us consider his feelings, no?

THOMAS   Yes, absolutely. And yet. (*Leading through with expansive gesture.*) Shall we not be better than his worst moments, shall we meet his – anger – despair – with scorn?

Some physical gesture/way of relieving his feelings.

GRACIE   I still don't understand why there was no note. I still think it's cruel.

DIANA   I, also, don't understand why there is no note. Peter loved his self expression it doesn't seem like him to pass up that kind of captive audience.

THOMAS   The action was the note. It was the perfect note. Language would only have been inadequate. He knew that. Let us give him credit for that . . . insight, at least.

GRACIE   What will we say if someone comes. And asks.

DIANA   Oh hell.

SIMON   He was here for nine months. In that time he got like three phone calls.

DIANA One of them from his mother.

GRACIE One of them from his mother. He didn't return that call.

DIANA That we know of.

SIMON That we know of. At some point somebody is going to call and we're going to say sorry ma'am he took off and didn't say where he was going, we were sorry to see him go but that's the way the young people are these days.

GRACIE I think it's important for us to have a . . . version of events. For us all to have the same version.

DIANA I don't want to – I agree – but look, whatever this story is we come up with I'm not, I'm a terrible liar it shows in my face. So just I need to know the story. But don't ask me to front the story.

SIMON (*amused*) There isn't going to be an interrogation.

DIANA Believe me on this okay. If his parents come, that's a day I'm on a run to town.

SIMON His folks aren't showing up.

GRACIE We don't have to worry about any of this if we know what happened, and how it happened. And if we decide this as a group, if we all contribute to it, it will live in us in an alive way and honestly . . . after a while . . . we'll probably remember that's the way it happened.

Which is useful, though sort of a tragedy, probably.

THOMAS Something beautiful happened here. Something terrible. Something mighty.

And the world won't understand it that way the way the world doesn't understand anything beautiful and mighty.

SIMON (*declamatory, scornful*) *Jesus.*

DIANA I don't think we should pretend everything was hunky dory.

MARI No.

GRACIE Do you think he came here to die? This's the first time I had that thought.

THOMAS No. No. Peter came here to *live*.

THOMAS *puts his head down and starts to quietly weep.*

DIANA He didn't leave a note for us do we know for sure he didn't mail one?

Bit of a pause.

GRACIE He didn't go into town. Not for weeks.

DIANA But in the mail pile. Who took that to town. Gracie?

GRACIE Yes.

She's closing her eyes trying to remember.

DIANA There isn't that much mail don't you kind of – I always kind of look at it, when I'm running the mail I'm just curious. About the human condition I guess. Handwriting.

GRACIE I know. I usually do too. I was in a rush. Why was I in a rush. I don't know why I was in a rush I just I remember –

A small pile of envelopes, I have them in my hand, they're on the passenger seat, I'm thinking about do we have enough money to get bleach and a new mop – and then I'm putting them in the mail box.

The phone rings.

Several times.

DIANA We can't answer that. We aren't ready to answer that.

SIMON About a million to one it's for Peter.

DIANA How often does the phone ring?

The phone continues to ring. And continues to ring.

GRACIE Ghazal?

Ghazal?

A young thin man looks up quietly.

What do you think? What do you think we should do?

He blinks a few times, it's extremely unclear if he's taken any of this in.

GHAZAL Pray.

THOMAS That's right. That's just right. Thank you Ghazal.

GHAZAL *blinks, extremely unclear if he's gratified by this.*

THOMAS Simon?

Do you want to handle this?

SIMON Yeah alright.

He kind of scrambles up, stands.

Reaches – mentally if not physically.

To you, for whom we have not found an adequate name

To you, who we struggle to see through the bad strange perversions of worship we were forced into by our parents, many of whom in their desperate weak way genuinely loved us; by society, which pretended to love us but most assuredly did not; these are the bad mists we struggle through to find you

We know you are the mists, as well as the struggle we know, we struggle to know

Somewhere in here the phone has stopped ringing, or maybe it's more that the clamor of it has slowly died away.

We're reduced to a world of riddles take pity

We are thirsty for as much of your grace as you will give us

We are your petals, yearning for rain.

Can we get an A

ALL (*with a tone, like a hum*)   A

SIMON   Can we have an M

ALL (*same*)   M

SIMON (*sonorous, lilting*)   Please give me an E

ALL   E

SIMON (*half singing this one*)   And then the N

ALL (*a hum, basically*)   Ay – men.

And then, without articulated syllables, the same hum.

GHAZAL *takes up the hum, and takes it somewhere else a bit wilder, and stranger, a hooting and a hollering – it is absolutely unclear if he has taken the moment and amplified varied and given it glory, if he is parodying and mocking it, or if he has merely been triggered into a world of sonics.*

By the end he might sound a bit like a wolf, **MARI** *is taking him, meanwhile, and gently leading him off.*

CHORAL – 2   Steel wool

CHORAL – 3   Sponges, gloves

CHORAL – 5   Brushes

CHORAL – 6   Sandpaper

CHORAL – 7   Teflon tape

CHORAL – 6   3-inch gate valves

CHORAL – 2   Compression elbows

CHORAL – 3   The tire holding down the blue tarp

CHORAL – 5   on the hot compost pile

CHORAL – 5 One crow and then two crows

CHORAL – 3 on the cold compost pile

CHORAL – 7 3 cast iron bathtubs in a row:

CHORAL – 2 blue

CHORAL – 6 red

CHORAL – 3 rust

CHORAL – 6 Deer spine

CHORAL – 3 Crows

MILO (*to the audience*)   The night it happened.

The last notes of a Triangle, dying out and heard as if from a distance.

THOMAS Where's Peter?

MILO Sleeping.

THOMAS Go wake him up.

MARI Let him sleep.

THOMAS Isn't Peter Grace?

MARI I can be Grace, let him sleep.

THOMAS Are you sure he's sleeping?

MILO His door is a little open so I saw.

DIANA Go up and just, gently (*To someone.*) I'd hate to fall asleep and sleep through dinner.

MARI Okay but if he says he's tired . . . let him sleep I'll do Grace.

GRACIE Do a short Grace.

MARI What does that mean?

GRACIE That I'm starving!!

PAUL Hey can we add woodstove clean to the chore list?

MARI Oh.

DIANA Paul, no, this is dinner. Dinner has to be sacred.

PAUL Are chores not in some sense sacred?

DIANA Dinner cannot be a House Meeting Paul it just can't be.

PAUL I've been trying to raise this for the last three and we always run over and

THOMAS Can't this wait?

MILO (*offstage, loud knocking*) Peter, you're Grace. Peter, you're Grace.

PAUL If we wait it will be a dilemma which is forever unresolved.

GRACIE It *is* a drag to go to start a fire and have to clean it all up.

SIMON It's a real drag to wait the whole fire through and clean it after.

DIANA But it has to be done.

PAUL Obviously it has to be done but I just want to say, it would be great if we can find a way to be conscientious about reflecting – in the way we handle that chore – that it's a messy unpleasant process and it needs to be . . . I don't want to do it and feel resentment about who isn't doing it.

GRACIE Can we count it as like a chore-and-a-half?

DIANA Or two chores?

MARI It isn't that big a deal honestly it takes [five minutes]

SIMON It's the fine ash aspect of it, the swirling about the uncontainability.

DIANA The dirtiness. The smudginess.

MARI So let's make it a chore-and-a-half, and see how that goes.

SIMON Chore-and-a-half, alright, I'm optimistic.

PAUL (*kind of a quip*) Everyone wants to start a fire, no one wants to clear out the ashes in the morning.

MILO Peter says he's sleeping.

DIANA You woke him up –

MILO I didn't wake him up he's sleeping.

PAUL If he says he's sleeping, he's not asleep he's in a twilight half slumber which is a very pleasant place to be but it's not asleep. Do you go right to sleep, or do you drift about for a while in a twilight phase and see increasingly strange and vivid versions of reality?

MILO I think I just go right to sleep.

PAUL Ah, to be young again.

MARI (*clinking on the glass*) Ladles and June Bugs and little weevils your attention please.

PAUL (*to* **MILO** *and perhaps including a few more of the kids*) Little weevils – that's you!

Agreeable child laughter.

ADULT MILO (*to audience*) I like Paul because he talks to me both like an adult, and a clown, and is a good and reliable rough-houser. Two years from now we will go into the woods for a chat and . . . even years and years of therapy will not convince me that rape is the exact word for it, but I am 8.

MARI *Unaccustomed as I am to public speaking*, and, having been instructed to keep this – perhaps the most truly sacred moment of our day – short – I would like you to direct all of your attentions firstly to the semi-bounteous offering which is before us, the fresh greens and the brown rice and the nice beans and the turkey gizzard gravy because turkey gizzards were on sale for which we give extra thanks – but aha not yet that's not all – because I want to give thanks for the present and at the same time I also want to give thanks for the future when we will be eating this exact same meal only *all* of it will come from our own gardens except maybe the rice.

SIMON   I think we can grow rice.

MARI   I'm not convinced but it's up to God not me and so maybe the rice too and I want to give thanks also to the past but that's complicated and would take too long to do it right, and most importantly, I want to give thanks to everyone here at these tables, to our Little Weevils all: Tanya Crystal Laurel Rolf Adam Milo Robert Mara* to our Ladles and June Bugs and: our beloved Ghazal and Peter upstairs sleeping too

look into your hearts and behold and rejoice gimme an A

ALL (*a short brisk*)   A

MARI   Gimme a M

ALL   Em!

MARI (*this is aimed particularly at the children*)   Gimme a E like a monkey

ALL (*mostly halfhearted*)   e! e! e! e!

MARI   and . . . an . . . EN

A . . .

Everyone joins in:

ALL   MEN . . .

. . . *then just a hum* . . .

---

* Very speedy and in a playful voice used particularly when enacting a beloved routine with kids

(*Ay-Men*)

MARI *Chow down.*

Like a WHOOSH or something?

The sound of a door opening.

PETER's *room.*

Women.

DIANA (*deceptively lightly*)   Alrighty then.

There is a fairly long beat.

This is just like women throughout the Ages, right? Washing the body, burying the body, then clearing out the remains of the dead.

There's a long reflective and sad pause. Then moving into the room.

These sheets – he didn't bring these sheets did he?

MARI   No they're ours and Liam's are just about worn out and these will fit his bed, so.

GRACIE   The sheets he died on?

DIANA   He died in this house should we burn that? Recycle recycle recycle recycle.

Wash and recycle.

Maybe wash them twice.

A pause.

And this is just like a man, to not hang up all of his shirts before taking his life.

GRACIE   Maybe if he'd been able to hang up his shirts, he'd have been able to move forward.

MARI   . . . I think he just didn't see them. Usually half his clothes were in a pile. I think it was habit.

There is a pause. They all come together, holding each other.

DIANA So we gather anything he would have taken with him . . . and we burn it.

Looking around a moment.

We need to burn what he loved best.

MARI I don't see what else we can do. You never know what kind of thing someone else will recognize. It could look really innocuous to us but

GRACIE The books? We're not going to burn the books.

MARI The books he loved best.

DIANA People when they're storming out they slam clothes into the duffle bag they grab one book two books it was Peter maybe three books. Max. One of them is a book of poetry, inevitably.

There is a shade of dark humor in this:

Find the books of poetry. Burn them all.

There is a moment of looking about.

MARI I think we can keep some of the drawings, the ones he might have left behind on the wall.

GRACIE Isn't it so strange that we're; I mean: rooms. We've talked so much about rooms, privacy, how much of that is a corrupt artifact and an (*Recalling the phrase.*) artificial property, and, and 'extravagance of space' but we still have rooms houses I mean I think that's how we've come this far I loved the first three months all of us bunking in the barn but after that

We've talked about rooms in all these ways but I don't think we talked about how your room is a temple to you is a home to the god that is you that is in you that is you

DIANA To the god you believe you are?

GRACIE This room was Peter's temple and now that god is gone and we're clearing out all of the the artifacts the, no, the the the relics

And not in the open air we're secret about it too in the wrong ways

It just feels. It feels so *strange*.

She starts to cry, several of them comfort her.

DIANA It feels really strange. We need a ceremony don't we.

GRACIE I'm sick of making up ceremonies. I wish we had one right here we could just *do* it and not *think* about it.

I love the ceremonies I love making them up

MARI (*correcting*) It's not making them up it's . . . *perceiving* them . . .

RUTH Right. I think what I really really want, is a note. I want a goodbye.

MARI Here's the ceremony we're missing – the god is gone, and we are deconsecrating his temple, right? So we can think about ways that temples are deconsecrated, churches are deconsecrated – I don't know if that's in the encyclopedia – maybe I can ask the pastor in town I can't ask the pastor –

DIANA I was watching Lula give birth last night . . . and watching the kids watch her give birth . . . watching her with her piglets and the care she gives to each one of them watching her nuzzle them and and . . . and relish them . . . and how that made the kids' hearts melt and I thought how is it that we cannot, will not say to his mom the person who gave life to him, the person through whose vagina he passed on his way to the world shouldn't we be able to say to her: these shirts still smell like him, would you like one? Don't you want some of these drawings? That's the ceremony we're missing.

GRACIE We couldn't *give* her anything. It would belong to her she'd take it all and his time with us would mean nothing. She has legal ownership over someone she had only physical kinship with.

DIANA Here's what we could give her: he's gone. Stop searching. You'll never find him again in this world.

GRACIE What we did was right. Absolutely it was what he would have wanted.

Brief pause.

DIANA Everyone wants to start a fire, no one wants to clear the ashes out in the morning.

GHAZAL *steps forward, holding a candle in a glass.*

His expression is blank, oddly blank.

His gaze comes into focus for one moment . . . he might see the audience . . . it slips out of focus again.

Then his gaze sort of – largely without moving at all – his gaze wanders and then focuses.

He squats.

Places the candle on the floor.

And pulls a sheet of lined paper from inside his shirt.

He holds it in front of him, reading it slowly and intently – we can see lines and lines of messy handwriting filling up half the sheet.

He turns the paper upside down and continues to read.

Then he flips the page over – the side we now see – which he has been reading – is blank.

He continues to read this new side at the same pace, rotating it around as he does so.

He stops, abruptly.

Looks off into space, rocking slightly on his haunches.

He looks again at the sheet of paper.

He paws at it slightly, traces it explores it with his fingers as if it was a puzzle.

Abruptly he tears off a small corner. Rolls it up into a little pill. Carefully puts the pill onto his tongue, and then swallow and chews, speculatively.

Another blank moment.

He looks down, tears off a bigger piece, rolls it up chews and swallows more voraciously.

Another moment of blank.

Then he goes after another chunk with more interest and even as he is chewing is tearing off another larger piece; begins to consume the note with increasing if still somewhat furtive appetite, cramming it into his mouth and chewing widely and vigorously.

Also late at night. **MARI** *and* **THOMAS**'s *room,* **THOMAS** *enters with a toothbrush,* **MARI** *is braiding her hair or something:*

MARI We have a problem with the new piglets.

THOMAS Oh god.

Automatically, half in his pajamas, he reaches for his coat.

MARI The kids have decided one of them might be Peter.

She breaks out in laughter which she then muffles because it's late, possible the laughter though not long does become slightly hysterical.

THOMAS They have a point. One of them *might* be Peter.

MARI Oh . . .

Peter didn't want to be bacon.

THOMAS I don't know that you have a choice, actually, when you remove yourself from the world perhaps you just decant into the nearest next container.

The Burning Cauldron of Fiery Fire 29

MARI   Well . . . it's an abstruse cosmological point, except. I don't think any of these piglets can become bacon now. I think it will freak the children out. They're pretty up in arms about it.

THOMAS   Unless they forget about it.

MARI   Yes. They might. Or fixate.

Lula is so incredibly smart,

and she loves these babies so much. I liked the toughness of this whole project the realness of it

but how can I break her heart

if I'm not desperately hungry which I'm not

THOMAS   She loves them now while they're cute and not so much work. She'll be begging us to deliver her from them, before long.

MARI   We should have hidden Peter's death from the children, we should have done a better job of

THOMAS   We're always saying we don't want to hide things from them and anyhow in the hullabaloo

MARI   They're going to talk about it you know, I mean how can we stop them.

THOMAS   Who will they speak to.

MARI   Anyone they come near the whole event was so remarkable from a child's perspective.

A ruminative pause.

THOMAS   We could swear them to secrecy.

MARI   I can't think of anything more likely to backfire.

THOMAS   If we if we make an initiation of some kind by torchlight someone dressed like an enormous crow or or I don't know and we say we say not that this is something they *cannot* tell but something it is too *precious* to tell.

MARI   The little ones won't understand it. Tanya and Crystal will smell a rat I know that for sure. And can you imagine, if any of them try to describe *that* ceremony to a stranger? We can protect them, in so many ways, but we can't fence them up forever.

Part of me thinks: are we no better than the rest of this country have we become a typical American family, full of dark secrets? And the other part of me wonders: wait a minute, how do they do it, all those American families, how do they keep those dark secrets . . .

THOMAS (*absently*)   Abstract forms of abstract terror. (*His real response*:) We did what we did for the right reasons I believe that truly and where something is done in purity, although there is smoke, there is a way through.

MARI   They're so little, you know, some of them, they're living half in dreams, which is why it doesn't really matter to them when someone dies life isn't quite real to them yet the world is so full of . . . stories, phantasms, miracles –

Oh, you know . . .

Wait a minute, wait a minute . . .

She ruminates a minute . . .

I. Have. An. Idea.

A beat.

THOMAS   Yeah?

The ponging of the woodstove. Patter of heavy rain.

The phone rings, the phone rings, the phone rings, the phone rings.

Maybe some choral sonics here? While the phone is ringing?

DIANA (*somewhat breathlessly*)   Hello?

Oh. Hello, Mrs. Rutherford. No Peter isn't here. I mean, he isn't here at all any more. He left.

She's kind of signaling around her desperately.

Well about I don't know three or four weeks ago. I don't know the exact date (*She realizes this is an unlikely bit of oversharing.*) hey (*Performatively loud.*) anyone remember when Peter left?

THOMAS *grabs the phone from her.*

THOMAS   Hello, Mrs. Rutherford? Thomas here. I don't know if you remember but we spoke – oh goof. Great. That's simpler. Peter left us three-and-a-half weeks ago, I'm sorry I can't be more helpful but he didn't give us a forwarding number.

Well he had mentioned Yuma Creek which is a – but

I don't know that that was a definite plan.

No Yuma Creek isn't camping it's – a kind of a community – I don't believe they have phones there but there must be a mailing address but – I'm so sorry just a moment I'm (*He isn't.*) checking – we have a cork board I'm checking to see if, no, (*Fingers half over the receiver.*) hey anyone here in touch with anyone from Yuma Creek? Is Brad, do you think? Doesn't he know that dome guy? He doesn't? Who did? Oh.

I'm afraid I can't be more helpful about that but if he's gone to Yuma Creek probably the best thing is to wait for him to contact you – you haven't had any letters from him lately?

Ah, well he wasn't much of a letter writer.

A wee bit of a pause while he listens.

Oh I'm so sorry to hear that.

A bit more.

Yes I'm sorry to hear that and if by any chance he does return to us, because he's welcome, we'll definitely let him know you're looking for him I'm putting a note up on the corkboard right now to that effect.

The farming is going pretty well, thank you for asking Mrs. Rutherford. Alright well good bye and good luck and I'm sure Peter will get hold of you he's probably just getting his head back together right now.

Alright well bye now.

(*Disproportionately wrathful.*)

When the winds took the line down I said that was as good as a sign we don't need (*Pointing at phone.*) this *thing*

I don't need to talk to a woman who doesn't know where her son is that's not the kind of person I want in my orbit *this*

is a gate from *anywhere* what good is it to be away from all that crap all of that mental pollution when a box can start talking to me any kind of a way smack in the middle of my *home* I'm subject to a federal government whose hegemony over this good earth I do not recognize and whose laws I find generally offensive right I know there is on some level no escape from this kind of invisible legal societal netting without an army and a vast liberation but I believe that being harder to break *means* something

I'm tearing it down right now. Because it needed to happen anyway. And before that frantic harridan can call back.

She wasn't going to say anything at this moment but now she has to:

MARI What if something happens to one of the kids?

THOMAS If something happens, to one of the children, or one of the adults, we will put them in a car, and we will drive them to the hospital.

DIANA If someone is spurting blood!

THOMAS Better they spurt blood in the car driving *to* the hospital instead of sitting here spurting blood while waiting *for* the ambulance.

MARI If they cannot be moved and must be immobilized

THOMAS If there's a spinal injury they're doomed you can't those roads the jolting it this is just this is a level of risk you take when you separate yourself from the umbilical cord of a corrupt civilization can anyone give me a compelling argument for a situation in which this object is likely to protect us from death because let me remind you that if that is its responsibility we have a recent example of it failing at just that.

GRACIE I don't want to tear down the line! I can't say why right now I mean I can't put it in words but I just feel like don't do this thing

THOMAS You aren't ready for it

GRACIE No I'm not ready for it

THOMAS Then there's still hope for you the change we're not ready for transforms us. I'm ripping it down.

He charges out into the night, the storm.

SIMON You know that's a way a person gets electrocuted.

He heads out after him.

Someone cries out, a few other people also run out.

GRACIE (*in despair*) Peter was right about us. Peter was right about us.

The kids: we will see them only lit from behind, dimly, as a stationary phalanx; some have flashlights. Fog, mists.

TANYA Wake uuuup . . .

CRYSTAL Wakey wakey Rolf

ROLF I'm asleep

TANYA Waaaaaake uuuuuuup

ROLF (*a little too loud*) Go away. I'm sleeping

LAUREL *and* **TANYA** Shhhhhhhhh.

Lines spoken on top of each other/all at once are indicated thusly, in underline:

CRYSTAL   <u>Nobody cares if you're sleeping</u>

TANYA   <u>This is more important than sleeping</u>

LAUREL   We've got to rescue Peter.

ROLF (*rousing to the necessity*)   Mphh.

Crunch crunch crunch of gravel.

ROLF   Waaakkke uuuuuuuup little Adam . . .

ADAM (*loud*)   Whaaaaaat??

CRYSTAL *and* **ROLF**   Shhhhhhhh

ROLF   Get up! We're rescuing Peter!

ADAM   I am not "little"

Crunch crunch crunch of gravel.

TANYA *and* **LAUREL**   Wake up Cookie Monster. Wake uuuup little Cookie Monster.

ROBERT (*whispering incredibly loudly*)   I'm awake! Are we rescuing Peter now?

CRYSTAL   We're rescuing Peter now. Come on.

Crunch crunch crunch of gravel.

TANYA *and* **LAUREL**   Shhhhhhhhh.

TANYA   Maybe Mara is too little . . .

CRYSTAL   We need the youngest because the youngest are purest of heart

MARA   I'm sleepy

CRYSTAL (*ruthless*)   We don't care. You have to help.

ROLF *and* **ADAM**   Shhhhhhhh

MILO   Where's the moon

LAUREL   There's no moon tonight Milo.

ADAM   That's why it's dark

LAUREL   Shhhhhhhh

ROBERT   I'm cold

ROLF   Be quiet Robbie and don't be such a baby

ROBERT (*half under his breath*)   My name is *Cookie Monster.*

Crunch crunch crunch crunch crunch crunch crunch crunch crunch.

TANYA   Hi Lula

CRYSTAL   Hello

LAUREL   Hello Lula

MILO   <u>Hi Lula</u>

ADAM   <u>Hello hello</u>

CRYSTAL   <u>Say hello</u>

MARA   Hi Lula

Flashlight, grunts.

ROLF   How do we know which one is Peter with all of their faces buried in her in her . . . vagina

ADAM   Ooooooh Rolf you said vagina.

CRYSTAL   That is not her vagina.

ROLF   It is so and I can so say vagina.

CRYSTAL   You can say vagina vagina is a beautiful word but that is not her vagina those are her titties.

TANYA   Those are her teats Crystal.

CRYSTAL   Titties.

TANYA   Teats.

ROLF Those are her vagina.

CRYSTAL *and* **TANYA** They are not!!

ALL Shhhhhhhhhhhh

CRYSTAL (*low*) They are not

LAUREL (*whispering*) Lula doesn't like all the shouting.

CRYSTAL It's okay Lula.

ADAM It's okay Lula

TANYA, **ROLF**, **MILO** Shhhhh. Shhhhhhh.

CRYSTAL (*solemn, explaining*) Okay. Now. Listen up you guys remember: It won't *look* like Peter because that's not how reincarnation works. You look exactly like whoever you turn into next but it's the *same* soul

TANYA It's the *same* soul

CRYSTAL And be serious because we have to save him because otherwise he is going to be bacon.

TANYA Because newsflash people: bacon is pigs.

ADAM (*irritated*) We know where bacon comes from Tanya.

MILO I love bacon

LAUREL (*this is about the pig proximity*) Shhhhhh.

ROBERT (*quieter*) I *love* bacon

ROLF Everybody loves bacon.

CRYSTAL Not me. I'm not eating my friends anymore.

ADAM (*highly irritated*) Showoff.

TANYA (*a little bit declaratively self-righteous*) I'll eat pigs, but I *won't* eat Peter. Nothing personal.

MILO How do we know

ROBERT How do we know

ADAM How can we tell . . .

TANYA The righteous could tell, the gaze of the righteous pierces through the mists of the world like . . . an arrow.

CRYSTAL Bring forth Mara because she's the youngest and so she has the purest heart.

MILO Mara

MARA I'm sleepy.

CRYSTAL Mara which one is Peter.

MARA That one.

Many Hurrah!

Hurrah we found Peter!

Shhhhhhhhh.

Hurray!

Shhhhhhhh.

CRYSTAL Wait. Wait wait wait.

We have to put this to the test. We cannot simply have blind faith.

Ceremonially:

Tell us, O Mara, ye for who the veils of this world are but newly formed, ye whose journey from the stars is as if it is but yesterday, O Mara . . . which one of these little pigs is Peter?

MARA That one.

MILO (*disappointment*) Awwwwwwwww.

CRYSTAL Mara, that's a different one than you said before. Look carefully and choose/*wisely*.

MARA That one.

ADAM That one is Lula. Lula is *definitely* not Peter Lula has been alive for forever.

MARA That one.

CRYSTAL Okay Mara is too old now I guess. But it's okay we have a backup plan. So okay the way they do it, when lamas are kid lamas, and they are looking for them, they lay out the possessions that were their favorite in their last life and the little kid sees them and feels like oh, oh, that belongs to me

Here we have Peter's favorite book of poetry . . .

And here is his favorite shirt . . .

And here is his favorite drawing . . .

And the piglet goes oh – I remember this one and he *goes to it* and then we know.

MILO (*impressed by the technology*) Oooooooh.

CRYSTAL But we need their attention and we need them to be not buried in her tough old *titties*

MARA That one.

TANYA (*tossing it off. Could care less. Very hard boiled*) Teats.

ADAM Paaaaay attentiooooon little piggies!

ROLF (*not mean but a bit jocular*) Up an at 'em pigs.

ADAM All they want to do is eat.

ROLF (*this is a joke*) They're such *pigs*.

MILO They need milk to grow.

ROBERT (*solemnly*) They need milk to grow.

CRYSTAL Well right now they have to save their own life and that's more important than growing.

ROBERT They all want to stay with their mama.

ADAM (*caressingly*)   This is a good stick.

LAUREL   Be careful!

ADAM   I'm being careful I'm just giving them a little . . . whack, whack

A medium sized soft protesting sow grunt and some little protesting squeals.

TANYA   Be careful!

ADAM   I'm not whacking I'm *saying* whacking I'm tapping –

"*whack*"

ROBERT   Be careful! They're little!

ADAM (*truthfully*)   I'm being very very careful . . .

Half under his breath:

"*whack*" "*whack*"

ADAM   There they go. C'mon guys. C'mon little guys.

Disturbed snorts from Lula.

ROLF   <u>Oh hullo little piggies!</u>

LAUREL (*to the piglets in general*)   Hey there everybody – who remembers this nice shirt? Who thinks this shirt looks cozy and good to wear?

ROBERT (*laughing hilariously*)   They're like little puppies!

Disturbed snorts from Lula.

Snorts.

ADAM   Cranky sow

CRYSTAL   Oh *you're* all right Lula, you're okay.

LAUREL (*whispering*)   Go to sleep Lula. Everything's okay. Go to sleep.

ROLF (*whispering with tension and intrigue*) That one is sniffing at Peter's book!

LAUREL It likes it!

Snorts.

CRYSTAL Hush Lula.

ROLF Hush.

MARA (*sharply*) Lula. Be good.

ROBERT (*though laughter*) This one is sucking my finger! This one thinks I'm Lula's titties!

Peels of merry laughter.

Increasingly disturbed snorts.

ROBERT Don't be mad/Lula.

CRYSTAL We have to find Peter soon you guys.

TANYA Stop saying "guys".

ROLF (*low*) Peeeeeter . . . Peeeeeeter . . .

MILO Good Lula, Good Lula.

Lula sounds pretty pissed.

ROLF (*low*) Peeeeeter . . . Peeeeeeeter . . .

CRYSTAL You guys we need to give Lula love.

TANYA I don't know why you keep saying "guys" Crystal.

CRYSTAL So what and shut up Tanya. We have to give Lula love everybody.

ROLF Lula.

ADAM Lula we love you.

LAUREL We love you sweet Lula we love you/sweet sweet Lula.

They're gathering around her.

ROLF Sweet Lula.

TANYA (*in a lilting bit of song*) Sweet Sweet Lula.

This is some kind of song/game/ritual they all know and fall into automatically:

ALL Sweet . . . Sweet . . .

TANYA Sweet Sweet Lula.

ALL (*some of them mess it up, but*) Sweet Lula Sweet.

LAUREL We love you, our Lula.

ALL We love you we love you.

CRYSTAL We adore you our Sweet Lula.

ALL We adore you our sweet.

ROLF (*kinda loud*) Peeeeeeeeter.

SEVERAL SHHHHHHH!

They launch pretty automatically and unnaturalistically into a complex roundelay/round/slightly unplaceable musical form:

ALL
  Our sweet sweet porcine treasure
  (our sweet/our sweet/our sweet porcine . . . treasure)
  Wise beyond all measure
  Your happiness is our pleasure
  Between us there is no fissure
  We are now/and shall always be/beneath the vast undulating tree
  Of life the wide unending/wide unending/world of strife
  The storm and wrack/the storm and wrack/and ruin of life
  This wild explosive world of joy. (Vast cracking shaking world of joy)
  Your sincere well wisher . . .

This is truly beautiful. Lula is not soothed by it, the opposite.

ADAM Lula's still mad you guys.

ROLF (*low urgent*)   Peeeeeeter . . .

CRYSTAL   Where's Mara?

TANYA (*automatically, low*)   Maaara

ROLF   You guys look!

MILO   Look everybody!

ROLF   This one came to me when I called him!

MILO   Look! It has Peter's poem in its mouth!

ADAM   It's eating Peter's poem!!

CRYSTAL (*the Pronouncement*)   We have Peter!

LAUREL, ADAM, TANYA   Peeter!!

ROLF (*I am the king of the world*)   I. Have. Peter!!

Lula is furious.

CRYSTAL   Oh . . .

TANYA   Okay Lula is really really mad.

MILO   Lula is really mad.

CRYSTAL   Over the fence over the fence.

ROLF   I can't I have Peter!

CRYSTAL   Pass him through to me pass him through . . .

ROLF   Oh, right.

TANYA   Go you guys.

ADAM   Come on come on!

CRYSTAL   **Who has MARA?**

MILO   Good Lula.

CRYSTAL   Go!

TANYA   Up and over! Up and over!

MILO Okay okay . . .

ROBERT Hi Peter!

ROLF Mara say hello to Peter!

MARA Hi Peter

Tiny tiny grunt.

MILO Peter knows Mara!

ADAM Maybe she still *is* pure of heart!

Lula is freaking out.

CRYSTAL Back into bed everyone back to bed.

MILO (*sing song*) We rescued Peter

The younger kids join in low and furtively but jubilant and triumphant as they fade into the distance:

ROLF, **ADAM**, **ROBERT** We rescued Peter, we rescued Peter . . .

Then all the older girls join in as well:

ALL We rescued Peter, we rescued Peter!

ADULT MILO I don't share the same set of givens as the rest of you. I walk among you, but I'm not you.

There's still a Harvard then and I go there and do very well I go out into the world and make very serious money pretty much by accident.

A lot of the time, when you think I'm agreeing with you, I'm just being polite.

But though your way is not my way, my way may not exist. I was brought up to expect something from the world I can't locate anywhere; I'm the holder of a question no one can answer to my satisfaction.

Sometimes this is a burden, but it's mainly an advantage. I'm never startled by the absence of a 'there'; I never believed in one. Major swerves don't particularly phase me and

I don't need to see the body to know something has come to an end.

In a time of change

deep unsteadiness

the crumbling of the foundations

I move among you –

Hand gesture – we may recognize it from **THOMAS** *–*

ADULT MILO   like a god.

Vigorous whanging of a Triangle, THOMAS speaks over it.

THOMAS   Who brought a newspaper in here?

SIMON   Oh man.

DIANA   Oh just say the Grace Tom.

GRACIE *(ripping the band aid off with an attempt at cheerfulness/chagrin)*   I did!

He holds it to her.

(*Taking it.*)

I did I'm sorry

THOMAS   We do have an agreement.

GRACIE   Absolutely we do –

MARI   This is not what the Grace space is for Tom

GRACIE   I was just – I'm going to whisk it off to my room right now –

THOMAS   And delay the grace it's here it's in the room I had to see it put it *under* something or better yet throw it in the fire

GRACIE   My newspaper my room.

She slips it under her chair.

THOMAS   I brought it up exactly at Grace for a reason

MARI   I don't like bringing this kind of energy into Grace

THOMAS   Grace is when we are renewed and restored and wrought in His name. Grace isn't always easy and that's maybe the most important lesson the Grace of God, which this ceremony of Grace invokes can be rough, ragged, violent, cruel a disaster

SIMON   Okay but how do you distinguish, then, the Grace of God, from . . . unproductive chance, malfeasance, or even the work of demons, devils if we will grant the suchlike a reality.

THOMAS   I think we can, I think we must, in metaphor if nothing else and apart from that well I think we see it all as acts of Grace –

MARI   I think this is a lecture though. And we have a dinner to eat. And we're using the word Grace in two ways, right, we're using it to talk about a really splendid and mysterious aspect of God we're talking about supernalism (*Explains that to the kids:*) that's when you perceive when you see or sense or feel God in the everyday. And we're also talking about a moment we take, as a family, to express gratitude, for a dinner which some of us are *really* ready to eat.

And which isn't just kale and beans is it?

DIANA   There was a disaster with the bread.

MARI   We can't eat just kale and beans. I'm gonna – (*Heads offstage.*) finish the Grace without me

Oooohs from one of the kids.

I swear to you it's okay with God I'm here for the amen.

THOMAS tings the side of his glass with a spoon.

THOMAS I want to express thanks, *fundamental* thanks, for the bounty you bring us, and some of that is material right in front of us: life which will bring us more life, and some of that bounty is immaterial – (*To the kids:*) which means it doesn't have physical form – and some of that bounty is freedom: freedom from cars and pollution and the noises of the city, and freedom from media propaganda designed to arrest the progress of our consciousness and provide answers to questions which are almost impossible to answer but which we can't shirk from answering and which we will never answer if we think we know the answer.

A

After an infinitesimal moment everyone joins in – some, particularly the children, probably join in right away but some of the adults take a micro-second so the first A is a bit ragged.

M

They respond.

E

Response.

THOMAS Are you coming?

MARI (*sliding into place*) I'm here.

THOMAS N

They complete the Ay-men ritual. There is a small perhaps contented residual hoot from **GHAZAL**.

MARI Peanut butter and tortilla chips and I put eggs on the boil and brought out the big block of good old government cheddar so go hack yourself a hunk if you are so inclined.

We are in the kitchen now.

CHORAL – 4, 5, 6 Cast iron pan 1

The Burning Cauldron of Fiery Fire   47

CHORAL – 2, 3, 7   Spatula 1 and spatula 2

CHORAL – 2, 3, 4, 5, 6, 7   Oven mitt mended with duct tape

CHORAL – 4   Cast iron pan 2

CHORAL – 3   Snail shells on the windowsill

CHORAL – 6   Matches in the box by the stove.

CHORAL – 2, 6, 7   Hawk feathers in a cracked Hen Teapot

CHORAL – 5   9 long wood spoons

CHORAL – 4   one hand carved

CHORAL – 2, 3, 4, 5, 6, 7   Cast iron pan 3.

CHORAL – 3   Blue bowl of eggs still dirty from hen butt

CHORAL – 2, 3, 4, 5, 6, 7   The kettle needs a scrubbing

CHORAL – 7   The butcherboard is scrubbed

CHORAL – 2   Bleached

CHORAL – 6   Scoured

CHORAL – 6   The stovetop gleams

CHORAL – 4   Plum stones in the compost bucket

CHORAL – 2   In the walls: critters

CHORAL – 4   scuttling

CHORAL – 3   On the roof: bounding

CHORAL – 5   scrabbling.

CHORAL – 2   Moosewood. The Enchanted Broccoli Forest.

CHORAL – 6   Joy of Cooking.

CHORAL – 3   A spiral bound Rotary Club cookbook from Medford Oregon.

CHORAL – 5   The Time/Life Cookbook Series: India.

DIANA *has just entered the kitchen.*

MARI   Diana this is Peter's brother Wilson.

WILL   Will. Will.

MARI   Will, great.

WILL   My full name is Wilson, I'm known as Will, but Peter made a habit could make a habit of using my entire name so I didn't know – which you would be familiar with. If any/either/all.

DIANA   Great to meet you. You'll excuse me won't you? I've got to make a run to town to pick up the mail.

She flees.

WILL   Great to meet you.

I'm sorry to just drop in like this I tried to call. But no answer. I don't know if you folks have a workday?

MARI   We do! Well we have several work days. Most of the men and some of the women are down on the field right now. But I'm here in the house today – I'm so sorry where are my manners what can I get you? Well water? Or tea? Or Coffee?

WILL   Coffee would be great if it's handy.

She goes off. She comes back on.

MARI   I am so very sorry the coffee is not handy. In fact it's fresh out. I mean entirely out. I don't know how it didn't make it onto the list this week but it did not but may I offer you tea.

WILL   Oh that's alright.

MARI   Does that mean yes?

WILL (*very slight hesitation*)   No I think I'm good without.

MARI   It's fresh mint from the creek, I should have said. Or regular Lipton we have both.

WILL   No in truth I was only saying yes to the coffee from . . . politeness I guess.

MARI   We really usually do have coffee.

WILL   It doesn't matter.

MARI   Maybe not to you but come tomorrow morning there's going to be hell to pay. We aren't a machine that runs on mint although I don't know, maybe we should strive to be and you're sure about the glass of water.

WILL   Yes. It's a glorious piece of land you have here.

MARI   Thank you. It is. We're grateful for it.

There is a conversational lacuna.

WILL (*really just making conversation*)   How long have you been here?

MARI   On this land, full time, almost two years. No, almost three years but um – we've been a community a number of us for 6 years almost 7

WILL   I wouldn't have thought . . .

Peter and I were really out of touch.

MARI   Yes that was – he didn't talk about his family much. So that was the . . . impression I had. I'm sorry we don't know more about where he landed. He had talked about Yuma Creek. I can give you directions if you'd like.

WILL   I've just come from there, well, this morning.

MARI   You were there this morning. You drove all that way?

WILL   I was there a few days actually. I had the impression, that Yuma Creek was not the kind of community to disgorge its inhabitants lightly. I thought it might make sense to give it some time and just, take in the scene, have a few polite conversations, see if Peter might trickle into view or someone might decide they were inclined to say something, point me in a direction

MARI   And no luck?

WILL   I ran into an old acquaintance my second day there and after that people warmed up to me quick also I'm so sorry where are my manners I come prepared to be hospitable would you care to partake?

He pulls out a small canister.

MARI   O – no, (*Cheerfully:*) thank you, not in the middle of the day.

WILL (*lightly*)   My apologies.

MARI   None needed.

She's opened the canister and reached in to touch, automatically lifted it up to sniff.

Wonderful.

WILL   It's called Bigfoot. It comes from a man who grows in Humboldt county and says he sees the big guy regularly. From afar. In the mists by the river.

MARI   They are not pushovers at Yuma Creek. You're sure he's not there?

WILL   Certain.

MARI   Well it wasn't definite. Just something he talked about.

THOMAS *enters.*

THOMAS   Poof! An Arrival.

WILL   I would have called, I did call.

MARI *points to the telephone.*

WILL   Is that your phone?

He leans in.

You have a phone in a gerbil cage.

Reads small sign:

"Strictly for the End of the World"

Oh – heck – that . . . that is a hoot. Or not. This is for reals? Is this your only?

MARI That's a compromise.

WILL That's a serious lock.

MARI It's something we're trying out.

THOMAS Well you're here in person now and that's the best way isn't it. Coffee?

WILL No, thank you.

THOMAS Did Mari get you directions to/Yuma Creek?

MARI He came from Yuma Creek just this morning.

THOMAS Peter make it out there?

MARI No.

A moment while **THOMAS** *is cleaning his hands with a rag or something.*

THOMAS I was hoping you were here to get the rest of his belongings, he left a lot behind. I thought he might be with you. In the car.

WILL No. How much did he leave behind?

THOMAS Fair amount. We've got it in boxes in the barn he went out the door with just a duffle bag. We assume he hiked to the main road and hitched from there. I think . . . we loved Peter and he's welcome, any time, to return but um, his exit was complicated, there were words –

Somewhere in this **PAUL** *and* **GRACIE** *have entered.*

WILL That doesn't surprise me. I think my mom mentioned our grandmother is ill, is dying. They were always close, when he was little, and he hasn't pushed her away. She's lucid she'd really like to see him. Keeps asking about him.

PAUL We're not hiding him, if that's what you're asking.

WILL No of course not. Just, if something else occurs to you.

GRACIE We'd like to help you. We really would.

WILL Do you think that I could, take a look around? This place, and all of you, meant a lot to him I know that much. I haven't, I don't know the last time I saw somewhere he *lived*.

THOMAS Of course. Absolutely. I'll give you the guided tour.

WILL I don't mean to take the time from your work.

THOMAS We'll work longer, at the end of the day, we're not on any clock but that of mother nature, or, the necessity of agriculture which as it turns out is a vast and demanding overseer. Speaking of which why don't you all head back, and I'll catch up with you a bit later.

People slightly dissipate except for **GRACIE**.

GRACIE What about that misalignment on the lower irrigation pipe?

THOMAS Check in with Simon he has a theory about that.

MARI *hovers around a bit ostensibly doing something.*

There's an extraordinary sound, emanating from **WILL**.

WILL Oh, hey. Please excuse me.

He pulls a flip phone from his back pocket and simultaneously sneaks a surreptitious peek at the caller.

Let me just turn this puppy –

He holds down the button.

Aaaaall the way off.

THOMAS (*formally*)   Thank you.

WILL *replaces the phone in his back pocket.*

WILL   You've got animals too.

THOMAS   We have six goats, for milk, a sow and now a litter. And chickens.

MARI   All the chickens the hawks leave behind, that is.

WILL   Milk and eggs. And bacon. Beautiful.

THOMAS   Yes . . .

MARI   We're working on the bacon part. We love them. We've come to love them.

THOMAS   And love is complicated and love is hard and flesh is a responsibility. They aren't pets.

MARI   Right now they are pets.

THOMAS   They are pets right now, and they shouldn't be, nothing should be a pet, everything should have its full set of responsibilities in this world. Let's give you a good look-see.

MARI (*lightly, almost merrily, as they're exiting*)   And this . . . is the kitchen.

WILL *sees a barred and padlocked door.*

WILL   That's quite a padlock. What's down there? (*Joking.*) Another phone?

THOMAS   The basement.

They're moving on but **WILL** *has stopped. Trying to figure it out.*

WILL   You're not cooking down there are you?

THOMAS   Cooking? No, this is the kitchen.

WILL   No I mean – look I'm sorry, not any of my business.

MARI   *Oh*, no. Definitely not.

THOMAS No that's not our scene. We don't put anything into our bodies which doesn't come straight from the good earth no processing.

WILL Clearly. Absolutely not. But some people, in a kind of impeccable as a way to finance

MARI *laughs in a slightly charged way.*

MARI It's an idea, but no.

WILL (*amiably*)   Right on.

Re: the basement, would-be-lightly.

Nothing explosive down there I hope.

There is a tiny moment, then:

THOMAS Oh. No.

Laughs and claps him on back.

That's not our politics.

WILL It's mine but I hear you.

THOMAS The boiler's down there and, you know: kids, fire.

GHAZAL *has come into the kitchen, he looks very abstracted. After a moment he heads towards the stove.*

THOMAS Ghazal.

Both **THOMAS** *and* **MARI** *are on point and on high alert; their high alert puts* **WILL** *on high alert although he hardly knows how or why.*

THOMAS Ghazal

GHAZAL *freezes, a moment, like a man who thought he was all alone in a room and suddenly hears his name. Slowly he turns, but evasively, towards* **THOMAS**, *like a plant turning towards a source of light.*

Enunciating probably more than he needs to:

THOMAS   Ghazal who is with you?

Is anyone (*Half craning around the corner.*) with you?

GHAZAL *does not move, there is a sort of heavy evasive consciousness about him.*

THOMAS   Did you leave your room, on your own?

GHAZAL *looks up sees* **WILL**, *stares at him a moment, penetratingly.*

GHAZAL   Peter.

MARI   Ghazal this is Peter's brother, Will. This is Peter's brother. He kind of looks like him, doesn't he.

GHAZAL   Peter.

He paws the air, as though clearing the glass of **WILL**'s *face.*

GHAZAL   Fire.

MARI   Yes. Peter likes a nice fire. Ghazal . . . let me take you back to your room. Did you want water? Did you knock your water over?

GHAZAL *stares evasively into a distance.* **MARI** *goes to the sink, gets a glass of water, holds it in front of him. Tings at the glass. He looks at it, doesn't reach for it.*

MARI   Let me take you back to your room.

She carefully leads him out.

WILL   Rough, man.

THOMAS   He came, with some overnight visitors about 6/7 months ago. They arrived late, said they knew friends of ours, which as it turns out is not true, and bedded down in the barn. In the morning they were gone, and he was still here.

WILL   So you're just.

THOMAS We're looking after him. Mental wards in California, well anywhere really it's shocking. 95% of the time he's absolutely peaceful. I don't know how he gets out of his room. He's gotten out a few times.

He's been abstracted the last part of this trying to figure out how **GHAZAL** *is escaping; he snaps back into focus.*

THOMAS We think maybe we can heal him. Through community. In Native communities a mad individual was healed through inclusion in the group, through love and warm focused attention.

WILL Which Native community was that?

THOMAS (*irritated by the interruption*) It's the first form of therapeutic. We may need to try a more . . . intensive . . . it needs thought.

Speaking of the barn, you were on a tour. Peter's room. The barn. A bunk house. The yellow house. The fields. That may be all we have to show you I'm afraid. We're a small operation.

WILL I'm grateful. And I'm about to trespass on your kindness a minute longer. It's been a really long drive today . . .

Microbeat.

THOMAS You are most welcome. We don't have a bed for you I'm afraid.

WILL Couch is just fine.

THOMAS Well then that's that. You have several to choose from. Don't pick the green one. We'll find you a quilt. We're strangely short on pillows. Let me take you up to Peter's old room and then I'll take you to the field as a starting place and you can wander as you choose and dinner is when you hear the triangle and that's probably around 6:30.

Sound of kids laughing and yelling and not for the first time.

We can hear the cadence – but not the words – of the We Rescued Peter chant . . .

THOMAS And after dinner. Well I'll let Mari explain. But before he left, Peter was involved in a special project with the kids. We didn't want to abandon it. It isn't finished, but we can show you what we've got.

WILL That Peter made with the kids? That would be wild, yes.

THOMAS (*he's looking ineffably kind of uncomfortable*) Well. When the sun goes down, then.

He gestures and they head out the room.

There is a small lapse of time.

Then a tapping, from the padlocked door. It is tentative but fairly persistent.

Then it stops.

Here is an intermission.

The barn. The light comes from all around, as through a lattice.

MARI   Whelp. Here it is.

WILL   That's not a lot of boxes. He left with just a duffle bag?

MARI   We think so. He did have a duffle bag and it's gone. We don't know exactly what he put into it.

For a while, **WILL** *is looking through the boxes of* **PETER**'s *stuff. Stands. Has a moment.*

WILL   Oh wow. Sorry. I'm having a moment.

We were good companions to each other, when we were younger.

I haven't. I don't recognize any of this.

The sheaf of drawings.

He didn't draw any time I knew him.

They're not . . . great are they.

MARI   I think they were intended to be self expression more than anything.

WILL   Do you think they're great?

MARI   Does it matter?

WILL   In a way, yes.

Pause.

MARI   No.

WILL *kneels down again.*

Picks up a pile of clothing bundles it up and takes a deep sniff.

Takes a second sniff.

WILL   Okay. Yes. That's Peter.

He's here in a way. Even though he isn't here. Weird.

And I can . . .

The bundle of clothing is still in his hand.

I feel like I'm touching him

He picks up more and makes a larger bundle and, still kneeling, actually hugs it.

Weeps silently for a moment.

Oh wow. Weird.

Weird weird weird.

I'm really missing my brother right now.

It's been years. Years and years. So long. Since I've missed him.

It's easier to miss him when he isn't here.

So long.

This is a very rare apology:

Sorry.

She doesn't touch him sympathetically or soothingly – this is respectful rather than cold.

MARI That's alright.

WILL What happened?

A slightly weird moment which he doesn't quite register.

Why did he go I mean. How did it not work out for him *here*.

MARI *sighs.*

MARI Peter and I, spent some time together. Maybe you would think of it as an affair? Only without the bad ethics this was in the sunlight, right? And for me, it was a way of getting to know him better, getting to know *him* better, getting to know another person better, not stopping at

Slightly struggling to express but finding:

an artificial margin for knowing someone

And it was wonderful. And it only became clear after a while – because Peter, although he was someone who could be very open, there were also so many closed spaces inside of him, just a lot of rooms –

That I felt what we were doing was an opportunity, and an exploration, and a journey

And Peter thought it was a choice. He felt, that I had *chosen him*

And there were just, just a lot of hangups and baggage around that, like, society but also

Also some personal philosophy you know, what he thought things meant or

So that was something I . . .

extricated myself from

I had to

A moment where she composes and gathers personal energies.

I so look forward to being a wise old woman

To having so much experience

Everything I did felt right the moment before I did it and then it often felt wrong while it was happening or

And Peter was broken up about it and unethical and unkind

And everyone sort of got involved they couldn't help it it was too interesting we have a lot to do here but that doesn't mean we don't get bored

In the end it was just, I don't know, a big storm, thunder, lightning, I don't mean that literally but he took off in the middle of the night, he didn't say goodbye.

Anyway that's that.

Bit of a pause.

WILL   That's that alright.

Bit of a pause.

Thank you for telling me.

MARI   I'm sorry this is all you have of him. For now at least.

WILL   Might be all I ever truly *can* have of him. (*A beat.*) I don't know what's the best way. If I should bring it with me and hope I find him. Or if he's more likely to come back here.

MARI (*simply*)   I don't know. He's your brother.

WILL   But you're his family.

The **PAGEANT NARRATOR** *is dressed perhaps as a kind of exaggerated/torqued Uncle Sam, definitely with the tall hat/striped pants and probably on short stilts.*

PAGEANT NARRATOR   Welcome! To: the Incredible Pageant of PETER who DIED THREE TIMES and came THREE TIMES Back to Life! Including: Acts of Violence . . . and Levitation.

Created and Performed by –

ADAM (*offstage*)   We *all* made it!!

CRYSTAL (*offstage*)   Shhhhhhhh.

***Music**, it's good.*

PAGEANT NARRATOR   Welcome gentle creatures who have been drawn from the dark woods to our fireside by the sound of music, and, *revelry*.

Some of you gentle creatures are humans, welcome; some are spirits of the wood, welcome; some small number of you are deer in good disguise who hope beyond hope that during some part of the merriment we will make a parade to the gardens and *open the gate* and in the torchlight and the feasting you will, before you are discovered, consume every vegetable and flower you desire which is of course *all* of them . . .

Perhaps a few of the children briefly bound by as deer.

PETER *appears.*

For we are here on this dark night, illuminated by the moon the stars flashlights and can lanterns, to stage for you the brief but absolutely remarkable story of: Peter.

Who made the terrible error of falling in love with a princess who was nice and beautiful

PRINCESS *appears.*

and made wonderful cookies and was really good at checkers.

PETER *and the* **PRINCESS** *are both played by adults.*

but she had a terrible, a dreadful father:

KING   My daughter will never marry unless she marries the man who is the pinnacle of all men

(which will be never)

Thunder, lightning.

KING   A ha ha ha ha ha ha!

PAGEANT NARRATOR   You see, he was a selfish man who wanted those cookies all to himself

So when Peter asked for the hand of his daughter in marriage . . .

(was it only because she was so beautiful? No, they had been pen pals for over a year)

The **PRINCESS** *holds out a letter she's reading:*

64   The Burning Cauldron of Fiery Fire

__Music__ should probably accompany this, and perhaps these words should be curiously amplified?

PETER'S VOICE   "I put my pen to paper scratching breaks the silence
When these words touch your eyes you drink them in silence

I long for the days I didn't know you days I did not long
I'm irritable, irritating, asked if I love: silence

The fog the bright of noon shouts passions move like a dream
Night rises the high moon streams down I wake in the silence

I longed for a well of silence, a cup to drink it from
I drink deep and dream of your lips moving in silence

Prayers are not answered and songs fall hollow and silent
Dancing beneath and between the words: your heart and silence"

She takes a moment, writes furiously on the back of it, reading as she does so:

PRINCESS   "That bird the fifth tree over shouts like a fiend, shouts
Some will call it sweet music I know it is a shout

Your words ringing in my eyes I dance through the endless halls
They nod, say it is grace and singing I know it is a shout

I submit a thousand times to silence and to prayer
The heart is a mighty hammer every beat a shout

The moon shines from the dark heights the woods shimmer with silence
Beneath the curve of the earth the sun waits to spring: a shout

This note is mute paper stilled words glittering quiet
My heart is an absolutely silent shout"

KING Yes yes, yes of course. There's only one – just a (*Coughing.*) *trial by fire* Minor Bureaucratic Formality you understand don't you? All the other suitors had to do it of course.

PETER All the other suitors?

KING Of course, of course.

PETER And they didn't succeed.

KING Not at all. But they were terrible men, the garbage of the planet. You will have no difficulty, I can see *that* at a glance.

PETER Good. Oh – there's just one more thing.

KING Yes?

PETER What happened to those other suitors?

KING Why, they ended up as compost in my splendid gardens! A ha ha ha ha ha ha ha! What an honor for them! One they hardly deserved! A ha ha ha ha ha ha ha.

But this won't happen to you. *You*, are *exceptional*.

PETER Great! I look forward to the test which will prove that.

KING Wonderful. Because here it is.

PETER Oh that's so fast! I thought I would have a little time to compose: myself, perhaps a poem –

KING What kind of a test of strength and (*She's slightly afraid she's about to stumble over this word so she takes it carefully.*) exceptionality would it be if you had time to prepare? Life is always unexpected and here we measure the exceptionality of a man – or woman – not on the examinations they have studied for, but the examinations they are *surprised* by. That, is *our* testing rubric. Page!

The **CAULDRON OF FIRE.**

66   The Burning Cauldron of Fiery Fire

*The **CAULDRON OF FIRE** is wheeled out by the **PAGE**. It is made on the super cheap but looks terrific, felt or fabric flames flutter upward. It does something incredible, puffs of fire or sparks wheeling upward.*

KING   Excellent.

Now jump into it!

PETER   Wait – what kind of test is this??

KING   Jump into it! What are you waiting for??

PETER   But that's a **CAULDRON OF FIRE**

A small group of fishies leap up from the cauldron, hang suspended in the air for a moment, and then plunge back into the fiery broth.

Are those fishes? (*To audience.*) Fishes are a sign of a healthy ecosystem. If fishes are able to live in the **CAULDRON OF FIRE**, maybe it isn't so deadly after all!

KING   Those are Fire Fishes!!

The fire fishies leap up again and titter:

FIRE FISHES   Tee hee hee!

– one of them emits a small spurt of actual flame – before diving back in.

PETER   Oh . . . shit.

From backstage: kid giggling.

MILO   *He said the "shit"!*

LAUREL *shushes him.*

KING   Jump, Peter, jump into the **CAULDRON OF FIRE** and prove your undoubted excellence and win your wonderful bride and her delicious cookies! Do it now Peter! Now! Now! Now!

PETER (*to the* **PRINCESS**)   Are you sure you want me to do this?

PRINCESS   It is the only way we can be together!

PETER   But it might be a way that we will *not* be together!

PRINCESS   Peter! Peter remember, before you jump into the

ALL   CAULDRON OF FIRE

PRINCESS (*continued*)   that you have something none of the other suitors had!

PETER   My exceptionality. I know, I know.

PRINCESS   You have my love. And love does not die. Remember that Peter: love does not die.

PETER   Love does not die, but people do!

PRINCESS   Jump, Peter! Jump into the **CAULDRON OF FIRE** and you will know the truth of my love!!

He jumps.

A long moment.

The cauldron belches.

A small spurt of fire.

The fire fishies leap up from the cauldron and then back into it:

FIRE FISHES   Tee hee hee!

KING   Page!

PAGE   Yes sire!

The **PAGE** *is played by* **LAUREL**.

KING   Go stir that **CAULDRON OF FIRE** to see if anything remains of poor Peter.

The **PAGE** *does so. He stirs it steadily.*

We hear a ringing noise, like someone circling a singing bowl with a mallet, or like a number of adept children

running their fingers around the rims of water glasses. In fact, both are happening.

KING It is empty of all but fire

We hear a faint high piscine titter.

and fire fishies. Poor Peter is gone. He must, in fact, be garbage, garbage among men. I had higher better hopes for him, alas.

And you, my fair daughter, you must be so desolated that he is gone, for although you are pretty picky, in general, I know this one met your favor. Apparently without merit. But you must console yourself somehow. Do you know what always makes me feel better? Whipping up a nice batch of hot cookies. Maybe you should try that.

PRINCESS (*composed*) Yes father. Perhaps I will do just that.

KING I'm glad you're taking this so well. Those expensive philosophy lessons must be paying off!

PRINCESS Of course, to make cookies, I will need an egg.

KING That shouldn't be a problem. I'm a king, there is a palace, we must have hundreds of chickens and thousands of eggs.

PRINCESS To make the best cookies, you must use the very freshest egg. Luckily, that hen – that one there – seems to be laying one now.

There's a small hen, over to the side, sitting on a laying box.

She is a cloth puppet, operated by **SIMON**.

HEN (*Lots of fussy noises.*)

PRINCESS How broody she is!

HEN (*Even more fussy noises.*)

PRINCESS It sounds like the egg is coming

HEN (*Very broody and uncomfortable noise.*)

PRINCESS   It's here!

The **PRINCESS** *goes over to the hen and starts to reach under her.*

What's this??

KING (*impatient*)   What's *what*?

PRINCESS   How extraordinary – she hasn't finished laying that egg!

KING   What?

HEN (*Many involved noises.*)

And she starts to rise.

Underneath her, is an egg which is growing, and growing

And growing.

PAGE   Oh no! The egg is so big, it's going to break the laying box!!

And so it does! With a terrible sound of rending wood

. . . and growing . . .

Until the hen is balanced, somewhat precariously, on top of an enormous light brown egg

An acting master class in very different deliveries of the same line . . .

PAGE   What an egg!

KING   What an egg!

PRINCESS   What an egg!

The hen coos in surprise and pride

and then thrums a little nervously

the egg begins to shudder and shake

the hen falls off it.

HEN Whaaaaagh!

And then after some impressive lurches a crack appears in the middle of it and

to some kind of musical accompaniment.

PETER *tumbles out, looking more than slightly wrecked and woozy.*

PRINCESS Ta da!

KING Peter!

PETER Yes I'm here . . .

Circling around a little disoriented.

I'm here, I'm here all right.

The hen makes a very proud noise and cuddles up to him, tangling in his feet.

PETER Oh hullo there good . . . hen . . .

She butts against him affectionately, he picks her up and holds her absently.

PRINCESS He's done it!

KING He's done it!

THE PAGE (*more for the sake of yelling really loud than anything else*) He's done it!!!

PETER (*collecting himself*) I've done it!

I really have done it haven't I. Amazing!

PRINCESS And now you see, Peter, the awesome power of my love. After all, it protected you.

PETER I mean . . . yes! Yes that's wonderful. Also I guess I was made of better metal than anyone suspected . . .

KING I suspected it my dear boy, suspected it from the start. This is wonderful, here, let us celebrate with a

He snaps his fingers at the **PAGE**.

KING glass of wine –

who brings forward a small chalice of wine on a silver salver.

you must be thirsty after your . . . unusual journey.

PETER Thanks!

Takes glass of wine and quaffs it down.

PRINCESS I did more than suspect it, Peter; I *knew*.

PETER You did. You did know. And your love, and your faith in my excellence kept me alive somehow. I truly love you and I am so so so happy to marry you!

PRINCESS Oh Peter!

The hen is very pleased.

They're about to kiss –

KING Ah ah – but not so fast. Not so fast my dear boy.

PRINCESS But father, he passed the test!

KING The first test.

PRINCESS There is only one test!

KING How would you know how many tests there are when no one has ever passed the first one? There is a **SECOND TEST**!

PRINCESS Betrayal!

PETER (*to the* **PRINCESS**) I'm not worried. I aced the first one didn't I?

Tell me, O King, what is this **SECOND TEST**?

KING The **SECOND TEST** is a test of great dis-cern-ament. It requires the testee to have lightning fast reaction speed, and great wisdom.

PETER Lay it on me.

KING You may use karate, judo, aikido, jujitsu, capoeira, or contact improvisation but both modern dance and taekwondo are *prohibited*. Light arms or hunting rifles, yes, assault style weapons no. The **SECOND TEST**: prevent the deadly poison from touching your lips.

PETER *is sort of running through this list with his lips, also he's started kind of half pacing and shuffling his feet like a boxer.*

As he does so he thrusts the hen over to the **PAGE** *for safekeeping.*

PETER All right bring it, bring it on – bring on the deadly poison!

His arms raised in a series of feints, also like a boxer.

Come on, come at me

He feints and half spars vigorously for a few seconds and then:

When does this one begin?

PRINCESS Oh no – no Father! No!

The **KING** *looks at his watch.*

KING This one begins a minute and a half ago when you drank the deadly poison down in a glass of wine

The **PRINCESS** *sinks down in despair.*

PETER Oh! O hey that's not good is it.

KING (*looking at his watch*) Any minute now . . .

PETER Okay it's not great but, Princess, please don't despair, after all, I still have your love, don't I? And your love will protect me as it did the time before!

PRINCESS Yes that's right, that's right Peter you *do* have my love and it is a real love and a great love –

She reaches towards him –

PETER *falls over and dies.*

PRINCESS Oh no, no, oh no.

KING Even you, Sweetheart, will have to admit he really flubbed that one.

PRINCESS Peter, Peter why are you silent? Why don't you rise?
The sun is high in the sky, my love burns brightly, rise!

Peter your silence is an explosion fog and smoke
My love shafts through the confusion let your eyelids rise

Night ebbs love gleams the birds launch into a ringing shout
Throw aside your silence join the radiant sunrise!

She is interrupted.

SHORT WIZARD (*played by* **MILO**, *the kid who went to rouse* **PETER** *during Grace*) Con-star-nation but you are making a lot of noise. And I was napping.

PRINCESS I'm sorry if I disturbed your rest. I was crying out because my one true love has fallen dead from poison. I said my true love would keep him safe. I was wrong to say that because it has not.

SHORT WIZARD Well that's because you, my princess, don't know anything about love.

PRINCESS Excuse me???

SHORT WIZARD Love is constantly becoming and re-becoming, perpetually unbalanced, revoltingly unresolved, unsolved, monstrous – a monstrosity? Monstrous – the one we love who leaves us: on a journey, or to work in the morning, or to another room and returns unaltered is not a real loved one but a charming phantasm of our own mind, a primal and primitive error the very devil incarnate love recreates us, reshapes us, it will never keep you safe it cannot protect you.

Love is too holy to preserve us.

It's obvious, fairly early on, that he's saying much of this as **ADULT MILO**.

He returns, with this line, to **KID MILO**:

SHORT WIZARD   On the plus side, I'm not only a very short wizard, I am also a very powerful one. Your tears touch me, and, I'm bored.

Whaps **PETER** *with his wand.*

Rise. Live. Try not to die so often.

PETER *wakes up with the kind of massive gasp people often wake up with in films when they've just dreamed something real or are transferring from one reality to another or just feel the need for more drama in their lives.*

PRINCESS   Peter!

PETER   Ah! Ah!

Looks around.

I did it again!

PRINCESS   Oh Peter.

Kneels before him, takes his face in her hands.

I thought you were gone forever.

PETER   Not me babe. Never me.

He's feeling kind of great about this, really confident.

Whatever happens, you and me: nothing to fear.

Sarcastical villain clapping:

KING   Wonderful. Wonderful work Peter. Wonderful. So glad you have it in you.

PETER   I really do, don't I! (*Looking himself over.*) I kind of had no idea.

KING   I begin to think you may well be worthy, truly worthy, of my wonderful cookie maker, excuse me, daughter.

PETER   I think I am sir (*Corrects himself.*) sire. I think I truly am.

PRINCESS   Oh he is Father, he is!

KING   I entertain – because I am a (*Stumbles over the word.*) scrupulous and devoted father – I entertain only the very smallest of doubts, and, for a man like you, it should be the work of a moment to convince me otherwise:

PRINCESS (*this doesn't feel like a performance this feels very real, very urgent*)   No! No. You *Bastard*

PETER *looks up at this alarmed (we might think it's the actor himself responding to something unexpected in the performance).*

KING (*still in the pageant*)   The work, of, a moment . . .

PRINCESS (*somewhere else*)   Peter – Peter listen to me you can shake this off – you can shake this off Peter can you hear me?

Holding out her hand –

I know you can wake up Peter can you hear me? I know you can. *Wake. Up.*

We already hear drums and thumping or some kind of noise.

PETER (*half distracted*)   No, I –

I can face this.

I want to face this.

PRINCESS   Peter don't be an *idiot*

PETER (*face flashing towards her anger a stand*)   I'm not an idiot

PRINCESS   Peter, wake up

KING (*still in some comic place*)   Ah ha ha ha ha.

*The third trial has appeared, it is a **LARGE AND MENACING BUT BECAUSE IT IS MADE OF SOFT GOODS AND IS***

PORTLY AND UNGAINLY ALSO KIND OF CUTE LOOKING DRAGON

*The **music** which accompanies it, however, is pretty impressive and daunting.*

PETER *is daunted, very daunted, but resolute:*

PETER   I can face this.

I can face this.

The dragon starts towards him, eyes glowing and flashing.

The booming of the drums.

The dragon advances upon **PETER***.*

PETER *pulls his sword from the sheath but it's only a paintbrush.*

The dragon raises its terrible arms.

With a flick, its claws become blades.

The booming of the drums.

PETER *cries out in genuine terror:*

PETER   Aaaaaaaaaa

The **KING** (*still in some comic place*)   Ah ha ha ha ha, Ah ha ha ha ha.

*With a gesture from somebody, the **music** cuts out suddenly and the mise en scène dissolves completely.*

SIMON   And . . . nothing worse than a half-rehearsed finale so we'll end it here.

MILO (*from inside the dragon. The Porky Pig stutter*) Thaaaaaaaaaat's all folks.

Low level tittering from other kids in the dragon.

WILL (*already preparing to clap though*)   We end . . . here?

SIMON   That's as far as we have gotten.

MILO (*from inside the dragon*) Always leave 'em laughing.

CRYSTAL (*a touch sanctimoniously*) You can make the rest of it happen in the *theater of your imagination*.

WILL (*clapping now*) Amazing. Amazing. (*To* **THOMAS**.) Peter wrote this?

THOMAS (*somehow slightly evasive*) Much of it. Much of it.

ADAM (*offstage*) All of us wrote it!

WILL (*to them*) I have not seen better on *Broadway*. What happens next?

MILO There's the big fight!!

SIMON Battle. Unexpected Levitation of the Hero. The Dragon crashes into the evil King, killing him instantly, and flies away slightly dazed. Peter marries the Princess, and they rule the kingdom. An undeserved but much appreciated happy ending. We're still figuring out the winch system.

WILL (*to the adults*) That's really excellent. Ridiculous. Excellent. Who is this for?

SIMON This is a complex multi-part gambit

THOMAS One. Culturework. Part of our Ethos.

SIMON It keeps the little freaks out of our hair for hours on end.

CRYSTAL Also we use math and stuff when we're making things.

SIMON Two, well two and three together is a Little Extra Cash and Building Relationships With The Community

THOMAS And for that purpose we will remove the "shit"

ADAM It's my shit.

SIMON And we're gonna honor the shit for home performances and remove it for paying audiences because . . . capitalism

THOMAS Neighbors. Because neighbors. That's a different lesson. Although not totally unrelated.

SIMON I think we should keep the shit, for the whole . . . wide . . . world.

ADAM I think we should keep the shit. The shit is real.

TANYA I think we should do one the kids do more of, right now, it's kind of like we're . . .

Trying this out:

It's kind of like we're tools for their propaganda.

CRYSTAL Yeah.

SIMON Whoa small people. (*Thinking it over for a second.*) Although this is not incorrect. Rise up!

MILO I LIKE doing the pageants and I LIKE when we do it together and you help us. I really like it when Mari helps us.

TANYA They don't help us we help them and then they make money off of us.

CRYSTAL That's right!

MILO I do too help! I do too help A LOT! (*Trying hysteria:*) SHUT UP

ADAM You just you just (*Is trying to express the thought: you act like a cynic to score points and feel important and in doing so exercise a weird power over people.*) you're the one who is the powermongerer YOU

TANYA (*outraged*)   I! Am just! A kid!!

ADAM You are a *powermongerer!!* You are a *TOOL!!*

SIMON (*the rhetoric is spiraling*)   Okay.

ADAM   I wrote SO MANY lines!!

MILO (*to* **WILL**. *Perhaps tugging on his shirt. Still dressed as the* **SHORT WIZARD**.)   When Peter died I woke him up.

WILL (*distracted but is able to focus on him generously for a moment*)   Yeah you sure did!

ADULT MILO (*to the audience*)   When I opened the door to his room, Peter looked over at me from his mattress. His eyes were bleary, and he had some foam at the corner of his lips.

He reached out tried to reach out tried to say something, all very slow motion, mouth working, fingers clutching, desperate for something.

I was used to adults reduced somehow, in the grip of whatever idea, substance, trying to communicate something they wanted me to understand for their own selfish reasons.

And I didn't think that was anything I had to pay attention to; I felt it was deeply discourteous to me, to my need as a kid to be taken care of, and to not caretake.

When I was a young teenager I suddenly thought again about this moment and felt horribly and decisively guilty; I blamed myself for Peter's death.

Later on in life I realized that of course Kid Milo had no experiential vocabulary to understand Peter as anything other than fatigued, or in a harmless state of incapacitation, and I forgave myself.

Some years after that I came to wonder if a different small child would have had another set of instincts. If Tanya had been sent up to rouse him, or Adam.

And one day out of the blue I surprised myself by thinking: did Peter remember he was Grace that night? Did he expect to be retrieved?

Did Peter die because he wanted to be rescued?

CRYSTAL (*to* **WILL**)　　We saved Peter! All of us did.

ADAM　　Peter burned up in the fire but we saved him!

They fall into this automatically.

KIDS　　We rescued Peter!

We rescued Peter!

WILL　　That's right, you did! Good going small persons!

He ruffles **MILO**'s *head, moves on.*

As they move into the distance some of the kids at least are still chanting the song.

Later that night. Outside in front of a fire, passing the bottle back and forth. There is some level of hush so that voices don't carry back to the house.

WILL *observes.*

THOMAS　　Did we decide to eat meat? Yes. For both health and spiritual reasons. Can we afford meat? Not really. Is winter coming, yes.

SIMON　　9 out of 10 pigs 19 out of 20 pigs at *best* would have trompled the kids. A mother with her young, a pack of wild apes – and she exercised a restraint which how can we not . . .

DIANA　　Yes. Yes.

THOMAS　　Sparing Lula's life because she didn't kill or maim the children – that sounds like something from a fairy tale rather than a logical ethical construction. I want to acknowledge that I *feel* gratitude towards Lula, deep in my heart. I acknowledge that she is a very . . . special . . . pig.

SIMON　　"some pig"

THOMAS (*buries his head in his hands briefly*)　　And I love her. She is soft and warm and pink and the expression in her eyes.

Buries his head again to weep briefly.

SIMON (*low. This is not entirely scornful*)   Oh Jesus.

PAUL   Lula is – well any pig – is as smart as your average dog, smarter, can we imagine can we seriously imagine looking into the eyes of a dog which adores us – and Lula does adore us we haven't we haven't been disciplined about how we interact with her

DIANA   I went to outrageous, and *personally uncharacteristic* lengths to to behave with her in a way which was pretty clinical but I think I was maybe the only one

PAUL   There's been patting, there's been cooing.

GRACIE   She was alone. She was lonely. She *wanted* contact

THOMAS   I love her. I love Lula. But we cannot make her into a god of our gratitude. And she can't be a pet.

DIANA   She has *years* more of piglets in her. If nothing else she's *useful*.

MARI   She's enormous and expensive to feed how will we get all those piglets to maturity we don't make enough scraps not nearly enough scraps. We didn't think the slops question through let's acknowledge that.

DIANA   Okay but we're not going to . . . (*Then, deliberately*:) kill –

GRACIE (*this is meant to make it worse not better*)   Butcher.

DIANA (*remembering* **WILL** *is there*)   The – that one piglet the kids have gotten really attached to, they will mutiny.

THOMAS   Obviously not. Yes. We will retain and eventually . . . rehome . . . that one piglet . . .

Lula is in our physical care but she's also in our moral care if we believe she has a soul and if we don't god help us we believe this is just a moment she is spending with us, and it has been a good one, and if we think her spirit is large and full of grace, which we do, we will believe that she approves and consents . . .

on some level (*He may be weeping again.*) to our good stewardship and caretaking of a larger project of which she has been an important and much beloved member.

The fire flares and rises.

Later. The fire has all but died down. **WILL** *and* **THOMAS** *alone, passing the dregs of a bottle back and forth.* **THOMAS** *is standing, for whatever reason.* **WILL** *adds a stick, it flares up.*

WILL   Did Peter tell you . . .

How much do you know about our family?

Do you know that we're rich?

THOMAS (*cautiously*)   I had the impression there was some money.

WILL   There's some money. There's quite a bit of money. Maybe Peter has blown through his trust fund but when my grandmother dies that's the first of what's going to be several generational transfers of great wealth. She's been frail and in poor health for a while so although this is sad – she really is in many ways a cool if formidable lady – it's also long expected.

A beat.

THOMAS   I didn't know that, no.

WILL   In just a few days Peter, a kid with money, becomes a man who is wealthy, and is going to accrue wealth and more wealth, even if he doesn't do a goddamn thing with the rest of his life.

A beat.

THOMAS   That's heavy.

WILL   It's extremely heavy.

A beat.

THOMAS   And he knows all of this.

WILL   Since he was 12, sure.

THOMAS I'm going to have to

WILL Do you need to sit down?

THOMAS Yeah.

Yeah I – I thought I knew him pretty well.

WILL You'd known him for, what, nine months?

THOMAS It was a long nine months. I have to

I have to rethink a lot this is bedrock

What if he's running away from all that what if he doesn't resurface.

WILL I don't think Peter has the stamina to run forever.

Look if he doesn't show up, after five years, I'm declaring him the family, the lawyers actually, will declare him missing presumed dead the money can't pool up behind the dam it's got to surge forward, march on, it's a big world.

THOMAS And it goes to you.

WILL His portion is split between me and our brother Mitchell.

If I'm . . . scrupulously honest . . . I'm looking for my brother alive *or* dead. I don't have a brother now anyway. And I know what do with money; there's a (*The very lightest offsetting of the word.*) 'revolution', and it isn't running on mint.

THOMAS (*takes a moment to hear him*) It isn't what?

WILL Nevermind.

THOMAS What you're telling me, it makes our endeavors feel small.

WILL I know something like this is a shocker, I'm not going to lie.

THOMAS It isn't the the fact of it it's . . . the language . . . where your heart is . . . located . . . in all of this, how practiced you are with the idea of great sums – it makes me understand, now, in a really visceral way, how so much of the world is shrunk into almost nothing in the face of the power which is the accumulation and amplification . . . I mean it's dizzying and I can't

I can't

I can't believe he didn't have the courage to tell me.

I didn't know he was that weak.

And I can't believe . . . I can't believe . . .

I thought we were soldiers together. I thought we were fighting the same enemy, together, and afraid in the same way. I thought we were losing the same war.

WILL (*testing the verb tense*)   Were?

THOMAS *looks up at him for the first time in a while.*

He has actually in this moment, I believe, forgotten what really happened to **PETER**

THOMAS   He's dead to me now. If he comes back, I don't know him.

In the barn. Morning. **MARI** *is arranging flowers into vases and clean glass jars. Each arrangement incorporates a few withered leaves and flowers among the fresh. Withered previous bouquets to the side.*

WILL   Oh here you are. I came to say goodbye.

MARI (*absorbed in what she's doing*)   You aren't staying for breakfast?

WILL   I should take off.

She looks up, smiles sweetly, but doesn't say anything.

He watches her work for a bit.

WILL   You're doing something deliberate here, I take it. Leaving the dead ones in.

The Burning Cauldron of Fiery Fire 85

MARI   Leaving *some* of the dead ones. The rest go on the compost heap.

WILL   Memento mori. Death is here with us now.

MARI (*quite delighted though she largely doesn't express that*)   Yes that's exactly right. It's all a cycle.

WILL   It's . . .

He looks at it from an angle or two.

deep. It would take some getting used to. I like everything vibrant.

MARI   And the rest hidden or discarded.

WILL   Sure.

MARI   I do too I'm – (*Concentrating on something.*) – trying to see it differently though. That's a lot of what we're doing here.

She works for a moment in silence.

He takes up one of the dead discarded stems.

WILL (*half to himself*)   'Death is here with us now'

He looks around him: the space, the yard outside and the hills rising up. He sees everything.

'Death is here with us now'

WILL *puts it all together.*

He sees.

She looks up and sees him seeing.

A moment.

I wonder if you might want to know me. A little better.

Without much of a pause:

MARI A part of me thinks: yes, I do. And then a part of me thinks: caution. And I try, I try to learn to listen, to that part.

WILL Did you think that with Peter? Did you ignore it?

MARI No . . . no . . . no I don't think so, no . . . I'm trying to learn to grow in discernment. I'm trying, also, to um to come to grips with, to come to an understanding that I won't that, no.

Closes eyes, concentrates, thinks.

I want to learn wisdom so I'll evade injury. That's very Western, isn't it?

WILL (*he shrugs*) It might be Eastern too.

MARI (*disregarding that*) But what I should be learning, is the wisdom to know that that the world is so wide and my heart is so wide or should be so wide that I'll *never* evade injury that I'm always going to

I mean if I'm really living, not hiding, living

I'm always going to . . . fuck it up, and, do the wrong things, and, have moments of feeling broken of being broken I'm going to break

I'm always going to break

And heal and break and heal

Until one day I break and don't heal, or, ideally, die.

He reaches out, and touches the side of her face.

She melts.

Oh, hello. Hello world.

WILL Hello.

MARI Hello dumb mortal coil.

He bends down and kisses her. And she returns the kiss.

The Burning Cauldron of Fiery Fire

The basement.

REAL PETER, *the boiler, the pageant dragon, the hen.*

PETER *sits next to the pageant dragon which is leaner and meaner and – not entirely real but realer.*

The pageant dragon ignores **PETER**, *but is a presence of quiet menace.*

The cherishing hen, as before, is sitting uneasily in **PETER**'s *arms.*

They're listening to breakfast preparations above:

These might be sequential, they might be simultaneous, they might be a jostle of both:

Pop of toaster

Scraping of knife across bread

Tink of glasses jostled against each other as they're distributed

Water running

Kettle singing

The chopping of vegetables

The peeling of potatoes

Snatches of conversation

Snatches of singing – all very partial, unintelligible, far away

Some dishwashing

The breaking of eggs

The frying of eggs the scraping of a scramble

Some kid laughing and laughing

The percolation of coffee

In the best possible world the smell of real coffee slowly fills the theater.

Bacon sizzling

A Triangle, calling everyone to the meal

PETER *cries out:*

PETER I'm here! I'm here!

The hen nestles closer and coos. **PETER** *doesn't notice/disregards her.*

I'm here! I'm here, everyone, I'm here!

A light hubbub

Chairs scraping

Juice or milk pouring into glasses

Glasses clinking

Dishes clinking

More bacon sizzling

More toast popping

More coffee percolating

More toast scraping

A knife tinks and tinks and tinks against a glass

Chair adjustment

The hubbub rises briefly, adjusts

Then there is quiet

Coffee percolation

Quiet

And GRACIE begins the GRACE

We can hear her voice, the cadence of her speaking, but we can't make out a word she says.

As her grace continues – spirited and cheerful – we come to hear – first as whispers, but increasing:

CRYSTAL (*in a lilting bit of song*)   Borage calendula.

ALL   Sweet . . . Sweet . . .

CRYSTAL   Geranium Horse poop.

ALL   Abandoned teepee made of dead bamboo.

With a surge of unexpectedly fierce longing and fealty:

LAUREL   We love you:

ALL   California!

We love you we love you!

Back to normal . . .

TANYA   We adore you Lodgepole Pine.

ALL   Cat tail, horsetail, Bishop Pine

They launch pretty automatically and unnaturalistically into a complex roundelay/round/slightly unplaceable musical form:

Foxglove, Lupin, Lavender

Jupiter, brambles, Mars

Miners lettuce, trillium

Poison oak and trillions of stars

Monterrey Pine Knobcone Venus

Hose couplers yarrow crows

The chilly thrashing coast

Cedar lettuce seedlings in rows

ALL   We are now/and shall always be/beneath the vast undulating tree

Of life the wide unending/wide unending/world of strife

The storm and wrack/the storm and wrack/and ruin of life

A SHOUT: This wild explosive world of joy. *A Whisper*: (Vast cracking shaking world of joy)

A whisper: This wild explosive world of joy. *A SHOUT*: (Vast cracking shaking world of joy)

Your sincere well wisher . . .

MILO Hill sage, Wild thyme. Wild thyme in a wild time. There was a time in my life when I prayed every day, when I prayed throughout the day I don't pray now and if you ask me if I believe in God I can't tell you no but I can't tell you yes. But I do believe in Grace, by which I mean: I believe we are renewed and rewrought and Grace, like love, isn't always sweet isn't always easy, isn't always deserved we don't always recognize it Grace can be rough, ragged, violent, cruel, a disaster.

(*Delicate.*) May I have an A?

From upstairs: an answering: A.

Can I have an M

From upstairs: M.

Please give me an E

From upstairs: E.

And . . . then . . . an N.

From upstairs: AYMEN

From the chorus: a vibrating and answering hum.

A bronze gong

And then:

The cadences of the Amen ritual.

Underneath this:

PETER   I'm here I'm here I'm here I'm here!

The hen nestles into his arms and tries to comfort him.

The dragon shifts restlessly and bumps in a cumbersome but meaningful way into **PETER** *who stares up at it with fear.*

The door to the boiler swings open with a loud creak.

The dragon swings its head in that direction.

PETER *looks over, in dread.*

Inside the boiler there is a fire.

FIRE FISHIES *leap from it, hang in mid air for a moment –*

FIRE FISHIES   Tee hee hee!

And then dive back into the mini inferno.

From upstairs we hear the:

AYMEN.

(*And then the hum.*)

The pageant dragon shifts about, grunts. Pokes at **PETER**. *Gives him a solid prod towards the boiler.*

PETER *staggers forward slightly, stares into the fire: horrified, mesmerized.*

PETER *puts the hen down, she squawks with concern.*

He faces the boiler.

He takes a resolute step forward. Then stops.

Takes a half step back.

The dragon shifts, restlessly.

From upstairs, clear as a bell:

MILO (*wating, contentedly:*)   I *love* bacon.

PETER *takes three purposeful steps towards the flame, gathering momentum as he goes –*

Blackout.

The sound of a larger fire, a gathering inferno.

End.

www.ingramcontent.com/pod-product-compliance
Ingram Content Group UK Ltd.
Pitfield, Milton Keynes, MK11 3LW, UK
UKHW051918220426
470276UK00001B/1